CW00566896

10 Steps
to Financial Success

Brian P Butcher

First published in 2013

Copyright © Brian P Butcher

All rights reserved. The author asserts their moral right under the Copyright, Designs and Patents Act 1988 to be identified as the author of this work.

No part of this publication may be reproduced, stored in a retrieval system or transmitted, in any form or by any means, electronic, mechanical, photocopying, recording, or otherwise, without prior consent of the author.

"I commend this book to you! Brian Butcher has packaged sound and straight-forward advice in a really easy to read and accessible book.

Financial planning is something we all need to know how to do. The thought of sitting down and reading a book on the subject may not seem too appealing at first. However, this is a joy to read. It's just like having an expert in the room with you, explaining it all over a beer.

Fantastic!"

~ Simon Hartley, founder of Be World Class. Author of Peak Performance Every Time and How to Shine.

"Brian's planning process really helps you to focus on what's important and makes sure you have the best strategy in place to get there as quickly and as efficiently as possible.

As a professional sportsman I know the importance of having a plan that will help me maintain my lifestyle long after my playing career has ended. Working with Brian has brought clarity and purpose to this and this book is simply an extension of his work and his character. I would highly recommend you buy it, read it and apply what he teaches. It can make a real difference to your financial future."

~ Ryan Sidebottom, professional cricketer.

"One of the biggest problems with financial advice is that it is usually full of jargon and business-speak which makes it impenetrable to us mere mortals. This book is different. It is written in plain English and is very enjoyable and, dare I say it, fun to read. It provides clarity and straightforward thinking which is rare in financial books. If you want to take control of your finances you need this book."

~ Graham Jones, Author and Internet Psychologist

"This is comprehensive advice. I really like the fact that it never flips to being too technical or swings back the other way to being light touch and presumptive. It is an excellent tool for the intelligent and interested user to gain a sound understanding of what is needed to plan their future."

~ Jon Lister FCCA, Chartered and Certified Accountant

Acknowledgments

Putting this book together has been a long process (mainly because I dipped in and out of writing it) but it wouldn't have been possible without the help of certain individuals who maintained their patience with me during the journey.

Special thanks, therefore, needs to go to:-

Brian McReynolds at www.worldscapeart.com for making me look slimmer than I really am on the back cover.

Martin Abonyi at www.sugarcane.co.uk for their skill and patience with the design of the book cover.

Thanks to Gail Powell and Diane Hall at www.thesolopreneur.co.uk for their expert guidance with the production of this book.

I also want to thank all my work colleagues and clients, past and present. I know you guys have taught me more than I've taught you.

Finally, I want to say a great big thank you to my family for their support and encouragement. Especially my wife for the proof reading and my two teenage boys for reminding me that I mustn't show them up by writing a book that's 'not cool'!

A Dedication

This book is dedicated to anyone who wants to achieve the best life they can with the money they have...and are willing to do something about it.

Foreword

Why write this book?

When you think about it, the majority of us spend a large part of our week working for 'this thing called money'. Many spend hours each week worrying about money and many of us, at some point in our life, have had a few arguments about money too. We can't deny it plays such a large part in our daily lives.

Yet, despite the amount of time, effort and worry 'this thing called money' consumes there are very few avenues out there for us to learn how to master it and make it work for us. In fact, in my experience of 20+ years dealing with the public and their money, it seems like it just boils down to whether you have a 'knack' for it or not.

Think about it, where did you learn how to master the mechanics of money? I imagine most of you don't really know, or you're thinking 'actually I've never had any lessons on the mechanics of managing my money now you mention it'. OK then, how about this question – where did you learn to drive? I bet you can remember that can't you?

You probably had a driving instructor, lessons booked in every week for several months, a theory test, took a driving test (or 3 if you were like me!). You learnt what all the pedals and the buttons in the car did. You practiced several manoeuvres until you could do them without thinking. Why? So you could drive legally and safely for the rest of your adult life right?

(Can you remember when you passed your test though and you first drove your own car without an instructor by your side? How great did it feel? Did you cross your hands on the steering wheel and rest your arm on the window just to be a rebel - or was that just me?)

Now let's just flip it back to money for a second. Surely, if we could just learn a few simple habits of how to make 'this thing called money' work for you, then the majority of the issues above can be overcome right?

How great would it be to know that you're in total control of your finances? How great would it be to have no debts? How would it feel to know that your loved ones are protected against catastrophes, your assets are growing and your future is secure? Sounds great?

OK, so where are the instructors that can teach us these habits like the ones we went to when we learned to drive?

Ah well, this is where there's a bit of a problem. Let me explain:-

Traditionally, financial advisers have worked in a way where they give advice away to the public in the hope that they buy a financial product that generates a commission for them. In theory, this may provide a solution to both parties if the product they buy is in their best interest. The buyer gets 'free' advice and the seller gets paid from an insurance company to sell the product. Everyone's happy right?

Well first of all the advice is not really free. If the insurance company pays commission to the adviser they usually reduce the amount they invest for you by the same amount. Or, if it's an insurance policy, then the premium will be slightly higher for the term of the plan to compensate for the commission.

Secondly, what if there isn't a product to sell or the buyer disagrees with the recommendation? Surely the seller has a problem now, especially if he or she has spent several hours working on your behalf?

OK, let's be a little negative here. What if the buyer doesn't really need a product but gets sold one anyway because the adviser needs to hit a target, cover their costs or just pay their own bills? Then this isn't a win-win scenario either is it?

So surely the answer should be that the buyer receives totally unbiased, independent advice based on THEIR needs, THEIR goals and THEIR concerns, that's not biased towards the adviser recommending the sale of a product - whilst the adviser still gets paid for their time and knowledge in return for making a positive difference to the buyer's life? Simple conclusion right?

Well, again in theory yes, but here lies another problem. In the UK there is a lack of willingness from the general public to pay for advice directly as it's been 'free' for so long. Also, many people still prefer to receive advice and reports before they make a decision, which is totally understandable. Many also prefer the 'give me the advice for free and let the product you sell me pay you commission instead' approach.

However, an adviser is not going to spend several hours going through a thorough financial planning process on the off chance that they may get paid. What you will probably receive instead is a quick fact finding process followed by a few product recommendations in a sales orientated report.

I'm not criticising any party here by the way, I'm just observing human nature from both sides of the fence. No-one wants to spend money on something that won't benefit them AND no-one wants to work for nothing.

So why doesn't everyone pay a fee to an independent financial planner in order to receive a holistic, unbiased report that focuses on YOU and YOUR goals and concerns?

The answer to that is also quite simple….the cost!

Due to the high costs and risks of providing financial advice I'm afraid that good quality and unbiased financial planning doesn't come cheap. The days of financial planners 'giving away' advice in the hope that they sell products that generate commissions are slowly disappearing under the costs of having to comply with increased transparency, gain higher qualifications, the increasing risk of litigation (hey, where there's blame there's a claim right?) and the costs of regulation.

Many of the changes to the way financial advice is now distributed have been introduced by something called the Retail Distribution Review.

Without boring you too much the Retail Distribution Review, under the auspices of the Financial Service Authority, has an objective of *'establishing a resilient, effective and attractive retail investment market that consumers can have confidence in and trust at a time when they need more help and advice than ever with their retirement and investment planning'*.

In principle, most of this is a good thing and I'm all for it - if the end consumer gets the benefit. Some of the outcomes of the Retail Distribution

Review are excellent. Higher qualifications for advisers, greater transparency of the costs of the products and the advice you receive, defined service propositions to clients in return for pre-agreed fees etc are all good at raising the standard and clarity of advice the general public will receive.

However, the problem is that these new highly qualified, fee charging advisers will probably not want to deal with Mr and Mrs Average who want to invest a few thousand pounds in an ISA or the young person that wants to start saving £50 per month they have spare into a retirement plan. It's just not profitable for them to give advice and then provide an on-going service for this amount of money under this new regime. Neither is it practical for the investor with this amount of money to pay high hourly rates to advisers. It's still not a win-win proposition for adviser or consumer.

This means that there's going to be a widening gap between those that can afford advice and those that need it. This is unfortunate because, in my experience, the difference that good money management can make in your life can amount to you being hundreds of thousands of pounds better off over a lifetime, even for the average earner.

So, dear reader, I've decided to write this book to go some way towards filling the gap that sits between the general public having an in depth programme on how to maximise their money and the costs of providing it.

For the price of a fish and chip supper I'm going to cram as much information into the next 10 chapters that I feel is relevant and suitable for the mass market. The contents of this book have been gleamed from over 20 years of studying and teaching financial planning principles.

The book will help you to identify your financial goals and then help you manage your money so you have a far better chance of achieving them. My one hope is that, when you read this book, you apply the principles I talk about. I've not intended to make the book a 'nice read'. I want it to be a template that you can work through chapter by chapter and eventually end up with a comprehensive financial plan - something which could cost a couple of thousands of pounds if you paid an independent financial adviser to create it with you.

When I recommend that you get a pen out to write down your thoughts, I'd really like you to get a pen out to write down your thoughts! When I ask you to get your calculator out to crunch some numbers, I'd really like you to get your calculator out and crunch some numbers! The reason is that I'm absolutely positive that if you apply these principles (and not just read about them) then your journey will be more enjoyable, less stressful and it will take you further than you ever thought it could.

So go on, get a pen, some paper and a calculator. I'm going to teach you how to get the best life you can with the money you've got.

Brian

Table of Contents

Dedication

Foreword – Why write this book?

An introduction

01   Chapter 1 – Planning your Journey

- Evaluating what's really important
- Creating your Lifeline
- Choosing the life stages and events you want to plan for
- Placing them on your lifeline
- Working out the costs
- Adding in likely receipts
- Prioritising

35   Chapter 2 – Budgeting

- The 'Bucket' concept
- The reasons for establishing a budget
- How to budget
- Establishing your disposable income
- Finding the leaks
- Focusing and prioritising
- Staying organised

51   Chapter 3 – Know what you're worth

- Why create a net worth statement?
- How to create a net worth statement
- Are you over or under exposed?
- Monitoring your progress

65   Chapter 4 – The Importance of an Emergency Fund

- Checking the car before you set off
- How to develop an emergency fund
- How much to save in an emergency fund
- Where to put your emergency fund

75   Chapter 5 – Ditch the Debt

- The downside of debt
- Ask yourself 'do I really need it'?
- If you're going to borrow then shop around
- Knowing the true cost of borrowing
- Restricting borrowing to assets that appreciate
- Why and how to pay off debts as quickly as possible
- Why you should never try to borrow your way out of debt
- Case studies in how to get out of debt

93   Chapter 6 – Build a House of Stone

- Are you insured?
- Why and what to protect against
- Wolf no.1 – death
- The need for life insurance
- How to understand how much cover do you need?
- Wolf no.2 – disability
- Critical illness cover
- How much critical illness cover do you need?
- Wolf no. 3 – illness
- How much income protection do you need?
- Wolf no. 4 – redundancy
- Other areas of protection
- Other points to consider
- Keeping protection costs down
- How to prioritise if budget constraints apply

117   Chapter 7 – Reaching your Landmarks

- The importance of getting the balance right
- Revisiting the 7 stages
- Allocating disposable income to priorities
- Compound interest rates
- Where to put your savings
- Saving is an A.R.T
- Availability
- Risk

- Return

- Risk/Reward

- Taxation of savings

- Making the most of personal allowances

- Using capital gains tax allowances wisely

- Bank Accounts

- ISA's

- National Savings & Investments

- Unit Trusts & Open Ended Investment Companies

- Onshore investment Bonds

- Offshore investment Bonds

- UK Shares

- Selling shares

143   Chapter 8 – Turning on the Turbo

- Establishing the purpose of your investment

- Establishing your attitude to risk

- The importance of diversification

- Understand the different asset classes and their risks vs returns

- Strategic and Tactical asset allocation

- Choosing your investment style

- Choosing investment managers

- Selecting the right tax wrapper

- Selecting a suitable provider

- The importance of reviewing and rebalancing

177   Chapter 9 – The end of the journey…or is it?

- The increase in longevity

- The pension time bomb

- Beginning with the end in mind

- Working out what your retirement will cost

- Establishing what's in place already

- Calculating the pension pot required

- Calculating how much to save for retirement

- Applying the right investment strategy

- Monitoring your progress

205   Chapter 10 – Review and Monitor

- It's a journey not a destination

- You have to measure what you want more of

- Monthly, quarterly and annual tips to monitor your financial progress

- Being patient and persistent

About the Author

How to get in touch with Brian

The financial planning workshop

Introduction

We're going on a journey. Yes, that's right. You and I, we're going on a journey. Exciting eh? However before we set off I just want to inform you about a few things-

1. We're going in your car
2. You're driving
3. You're paying for the fuel
4. You're deciding where we're going
5. I will be your co-pilot and the mechanic

The reason for stating this at the beginning of this book is because planning your finances is like planning a journey - you start with a destination in mind and then work backwards to create the strategy to help you get there as easily (and usually as quickly) as possible.

Imagine this scenario for a moment. I rush into your house and tell you that you HAVE to be somewhere that you've never been before, it's around 3 hours' drive away and you need to be there in 3 hours 30 minutes. I then tell you it's a matter of life or death give you the address and wish you 'good luck'!

What are you going to do? Are you going to just get in the car and drive around and hope you get there? Maybe you have an idea what direction it is and so you could simply head that way and see if you stumble upon it? Perhaps you'd go next door and ask your neighbour if they knew the way? Well that's a bit better, but if they've never been to that address they're not going to be too much help are they?

OK, assuming none of the above are sensible options, then is it more reasonable to suggest that you would get out the road atlas or maybe punch it in the sat nav? Once you'd done that is it also reasonable to assume that you might do the customary bathroom trip, get your wallet out to check if you have some cash, get in the car and check the fuel gauge? If you had a little more time would you check the oil? Maybe take a pork pie out of the fridge so you don't have to be robbed at the service station? I think this is more likely don't you?

What I'm saying is this, when you need to get somewhere you want to go, you would do some preparation beforehand wouldn't you? In other words - **you'd plan it.**

So if that's how we plan a car journey then why don't we do that with our lives? Or more to the point, why don't we do that with our finances so it helps us to get where we want in life? After all, life is not a rehearsal is it?

I believe the main reason why people don't live the best life they can with the money they've got is this - they simply don't plan.

Oh sure, ask them what they'd like to see in their future and they can come up with all sorts of things - family security, travel, a new car every 3 years, a holiday home, you name it and they've thought about it.

Life is not a rehearsal

The problem is that very few people sit down and transfer these thoughts from their head into a workable plan that will help them achieve their goals.

Can you imagine a builder trying to build you a house if your design is 'in your mind'? He wouldn't be able to start would he? Likewise, just having the thought of acquiring a comfortable financial future is not enough. All thoughts and ideas need a plan and a structure for them to come to life and, importantly, it's this structure that then drives the action and the discipline to make it happen.

I'm sure you've heard the saying "if you do what you've always done you'll get what you've always got?" Well this book aims to make you think about changing your thoughts, your actions and thus your habits so that your future will also change – for the better. This book, therefore, is about getting more life for your money.

There are also other benefits of having a financial plan that's integrated with your goals. Have a look at some of the findings of the 'Value of Financial Planning study' which was conducted by The Strategic Counsel and commissioned by Financial Planning Standards Council (FPSC) in Toronto, Canada -

Canadians who have engaged in comprehensive, integrated financial planning are significantly more optimistic about their personal wellbeing as compared with those who have not. Individuals with comprehensive, integrated plans feel better prepared to deal with financial emergencies and manage through difficult economic times, and are more confident about reaching a wide spectrum of life goals.

Furthermore, there is measureable proof that those who have engaged in only piece-meal, "as needed" financial advice are being left behind by Canadians engaged in comprehensive, integrated planning.

If you fail to plan, you are planning to fail

The interesting thing is that the first phase of this five year study was conducted during one of the most difficult, economic periods in Canada's recent history (between August 7, 2009 and January 21, 2010).

So, how do you go about creating one of these 'comprehensive financial plans that make you better off as well as feeling more optimistic and confident about your future? How do we achieve this 'increased optimism about our personal wellbeing', this 'confidence in achieving a wide spectrum of goals'?

Well throughout each chapter I will aim to give you clear instructions on how to create your own financial plan, make the most of your finances, avoid the most common mistakes people make and, ultimately, help you achieve more with what you've got.

I will try and avoid technical jargon wherever possible and focus on 'financial planning' issues more than 'financial advice' issues. Financial planning is essentially the construction of strategies or calculations that will help you achieve your goals. Financial advice is more about which products, services and investment fund choices to use to help you best achieve the strategy.

Some chapters will include both financial planning AND financial advice, due to the nature of the subject matter at hand, but one thing remains constant. By following the 10 steps in this book you can literally improve your financial position by hundreds of thousands of pounds in the long term. I know because I've done it with my clients, many times.

Whilst the majority of this book is aimed at the UK market, and therefore takes into account the products available in the UK as well as the current legislation, the teachings in this book will translate across all countries and continents because the principles are the same wherever you go.

However, as with all noble efforts there are a few obstacles or challenges to deal with first. I call them the 3 enemies of financial success. Let's have a look at these as early as possible so we know how to deal with them.

Enemy 1 – Laziness.

Let's be honest here, most of us are inherently lazy. If there's a hard way and an easy way to do something, it's human nature to choose the easy way. We would all rather plonk ourselves down on the settee and stare at the TV after a hard day's work than get out the pen and paper to make a financial plan right?

Yet when you think about it most adults are willing to get up at 7am in the morning, dress for work, get stuck in traffic on the way to work, do an 8 hour shift, get stuck in traffic on the way back from work before they can relax. Surely then it makes sense to just spend the odd 60 minutes planning how to make best effect of the money they've received for that full month's work?

In life, it's so easy to just start drifting rather than heading somewhere on purpose. It's as if the path of least resistance slowly creeps up on us and all the goals we had in our late teens and early twenties simply get lost under the duties of making ends meet, paying the bills and simply surviving from one pay day to another. On the other hand, those folk that are fortunate to have lots of disposable income seem to just waste more.

As mentioned already financial planning is akin to planning a car journey. When we get in a car we almost always have a specific destination in mind. We automatically look at the fuel gauge and assess if we have enough. We usually know how long it's going to take us to get there. Probably even have an idea of how much it will cost in fuel. We know which route to take and, nine times out of 10, it will be the shortest.

What I'm getting at is that planning is not that difficult. It just takes a bit of thought, then action and then discipline to stay on track. You do it in other areas of your life so why not transfer those skills to planning your financial life too?

Enemy no. 2 - Ignorance.

The other day I helped my son with his maths homework. We were doing angles! I vaguely remembered learning this at school when I was 11. The thing that made me laugh was that I can NEVER EVER remember when this came in handy for my financial future. For those of you, like me, that didn't choose architecture or geometry as a profession here's a reminder –

If the edge length of a regular dodecahedron is a, the radius of a

circumscribed sphere (one that touches the dodecahedron at all vertices) is

$$Ru = \frac{a}{4} \left(\sqrt{15} + \sqrt{3} \right) \sim 1.401258538 - a$$

There you go, you forgot how valuable that was didn't you? You can't complain about spending a tenner on this book now with quality information like that can you?

OK I appreciate I'm being a little sarcastic here to our school system but, as a practical man, I still think that the only people who REALLY needed to know about the Battle of Hastings in 1066 were the people who lived there in 1065!

So while I say that ignorance is enemy no. 2 in financial planning I'm not referring to ignorance as in 'rude', or 'bad attitude'. I'm referring to ignorance as 'lacking knowledge or information as to a particular subject or fact'. We simply don't get taught this stuff sufficiently.

Now I believe the curriculum will probably have changed quite a bit since 1982 but I'm still not aware of whole terms being dedicated to financial management, debt and planning for your financial future. Yet it's these issues that become a part of our everyday life once we venture into the big bad world – unlike dodecahedrons!

What I want to do in this book is give you a step by step process of how to put a comprehensive financial plan in place so you can't claim ignorance anymore and receive the benefits stated above that comes with having control of your financial future!

Enemy no. 3 - Fear

You may ask "what if it doesn't work for me?" Well, at the very worst the least that'll happen is you'll end up in the same place you would if you didn't plan. So you can't lose really can you? Let's be a little optimistic and assume that you'll achieve a little more than if you didn't plan. Would it still be worth it for a relatively modest time input? OK, please forgive me now for having the audacity to suggest you'll achieve so much more. Would it be worth it then? Of course it would.

If you are the type of person that finds it hard to get motivated to achieve something then think of it another way, how would you like your life NOT to pan out?

Imagine this (you'll find you do a lot of imagining in this book). You're 80 years old and sat having a celebratory meal with your 21 year old grandson. He's just graduated from university and is excited about all the opportunities the world has to offer, he's talking about travelling, getting a career, meeting new people, he's just excited about life. Then, after walloping down his pudding in a world record time, he stops...looks at you quizzically and asks YOU about all YOUR accomplishments and special memories that you've experienced in your life.

Here's my question. What will you be telling him? Will it be 'not much kid?' Will it be 'well I never had the opportunities?' Maybe it's the old 'I had responsibilities son'? Or would you get your list out of your life goals with all the boxes ticked?

You get the idea? **The idea that you're only here once and life is what you make it…and that what you make it is often down to how you plan it?** Well I hope so as this book will be quite pointless if there's nothing you want to achieve!!

The good thing about the planning is that it can be the most fun. It's also quite easy! There's no secret to it. In fact you'll probably realise how simple the initial financial planning process is and ask yourself why you haven't done this before.

Right, it's now time to switch on your mental sat nav, stop being lazy, stop worrying about failure and prepare for a great journey, the journey of getting the best life you can with the money you've got.

Remember though, to achieve this you will have to do some work. I'm only the co-pilot remember? It's your car, you're driving, you're putting in the fuel, you're deciding where we are going and if we don't get there it will be because of you! So come on then, let's get cracking!

Chapter 1 – Planning your Journey

"Would you tell me, please, which way I ought to go from here?"

"That depends a good deal on where you want to get to," said the Cat.

"I don't much care where--" said Alice.

"Then it doesn't matter which way you go," said the Cat

~Lewis Carroll, Alice in Wonderland

I suppose the passage above is just another way of saying 'if you don't know where you're going then you probably won't like where you end up! So whilst it's possible to get in your car and just drive around, this isn't the best way to help you get the most out of a journey.

At least if you start with a destination in mind you can then work out the preferred route of getting there. The route you choose doesn't have to be the same for everyone too. For those who have plenty of time to kill it may be the most scenic. For those that haven't it may be the quickest or shortest route that proves to be the most attractive. For the nervous drivers it could be any route that avoids traffic jams or motorways. The key is, if you know where you want to end up, you can plot the journey, and make the best use of the trip.

For the very same reason, knowing where you want to go in your life is vital if you want to create a meaningful financial plan for you and your family. Now when I say create I don't mean apply. We'll be doing that in the next chapters. Creating is simply establishing your vision.

Where do you want to go?

Stephen Covey states that habit no.2 of highly effective people is 'Beginning with the end in mind'. In his book 'The 7 habits of highly effective people', he states that all things are created twice.

There's a mental or first creation, and a physical or second creation.

This chapter, therefore, deals with the first creation - the one in your mind.

This chapter will take you through a 7 step process that will enable you to create your ideal future in your mind, and then we're going to transfer that onto paper so you can literally see what it looks like.

Effectively, we're going to create the journey that YOU want to go on.

The 7 initial planning steps are as follows –

1. Evaluate what's really important

2. Create your lifeline

3. Decide on the life stages and events you want to plan for

4. Place them on your lifeline

5. Work out the costs

6. Add in likely receipts

7. Prioritise

1. Evaluate what's really important.

The first stage in managing your finances in a way that helps you to achieve your goals is to have a clear idea of your value's and priorities in life. If you're going to create a plan

"Money is simply a tool that you use to exchange for products or services that you need or want to buy to improve your life".

that brings peace of mind then we first need to evaluate what's important to you/your family and then write it down.

This is something I want to establish as early as possible – money will not necessarily make you happy. If money made you happy then surely the richest people in the world would be the happiest?

If having money in itself made you happy then you wouldn't see rich people committing suicide or 'escaping' from reality by taking drugs. If money made you happy then 'The Priory' rehabilitation centre would have a seriously flawed business plan!

I genuinely pray that this book won't motivate you just to amass money and/or things just for the sake of it. My aim is to help you uncover what's important and valuable to you so you can then manage your finances in a way that helps you be more productive and fulfilled in those areas.

Your self-worth will always be more valuable than your net- worth and, in my opinion, probably the best £1 you spend will be the one where you help someone less fortunate than yourself.

However, if the way you're managing money today means that you never have a penny spare to contribute towards what really makes you (and others) happy then how on earth will you enjoy the peace of mind that freedom from financial troubles will bring.

You see, just focusing on the money itself will distort your viewpoint. It can also create an unbalance that could effectively make you less happy if you think about it? Jacob Needleman, the American philosopher say's *"Greed is inevitable in the absence of an inner aim."*

Remember the film 'Scrooge'? This is a great example of someone who got his priorities wrong by putting money before faith, family and friendships. Was he happier before or after his 'ghostly' experiences? If you don't know watch the film (or wait until Christmas as it'll be on then for sure).

However, please note that I said money will not 'necessarily' make you happy. I put the word necessarily in because modern studies are showing that, whilst money in itself will not make you happy, the way you spend it might.

A recent experiment in Canada gave money away to a large array of students. The amount of money the students received varied between $5 and $20 and the students were separated into two groups. One group was instructed to spend the money on themselves. The others were instructed to spend the money on someone else. Before they spent the money they were also asked what their happiness levels were.

At the end of that day they were then asked how they spent the money and how it affected their happiness levels. 2 outcomes were found:-

1. The people who spent the money on someone else reported increased feelings of happiness. The people who spent the money on themselves reported that they didn't feel any significant difference.

2. It didn't make any difference whether the money they received was $5 or $20. What mattered was not how much they spent, but the fact that they spent it on someone else.

The experiment then was extended to Uganda to see if the level of affluence of the participants affected the results. Guess what? Same results!

So, when thinking about the 'money and happiness' equation it's proven that just spending money on yourself can make you less sociable and more selfish, and both of these traits lead to you being less happy overall.

We are made as social creatures so the idea of winning the lottery and buying a deserted island just for yourself will probably end in misery and leave you wanting to exchange your money and your beautiful island for more friendships.

However, you could do what Richard Branson did and turn your private island into a place of hospitality, fun and friendships. Now there you have the best of both worlds!

By the way Richard, if you're reading this, I'd just like to let you know that my family and I would be very happy to accept an invite to Necker Island (well if you don't ask you don't get do you?)

Finally, one more point on this subject. When you do spend money on yourself studies are showing that spending it on experiences rather than material things has a greater impact on your spirit of well- being. These can even be shown when analysing the neurons in your brain that measure the 'happiness factor'.

So when creating your own financial plan I suggest you first spend time to establish what REALLY is important to you. You need to find out what your values are in life. What 'makes you tick'? What gets your emotions stirred when you think about it? Who else is important to you? You need to know this so that your financial plan will incorporate them. This is what you should be looking to spend your money on.

One of the best ways I've found to establish what really is important is to ask yourself some challenging questions that have been devised by an early founder of lifestyle financial planning, George Kinder. George runs an organisation called the Kinder Institute which helps financial planners to assist clients to integrate their money management with what's REALLY important to them. George poses 3 questions to help people clarify this.

However, before I ask you them I want you to go get a pen and paper and put the kettle on. If you're married do this together. You might find it interesting to discover your partner's answers (plus a coherent financial plan should take into account both partners' needs).

Have you got your pen and paper? (I bet about 5% has but I can't really wait for the other 95% as we won't get anywhere).

OK, let's have a look at 3 questions designed to help you establish what's really important in your life;-

Question 1

Imagine you had the wealth of Bill Gates. Money is no object. You don't even need to work as the interest you receive on your money each day is probably more than you can spend any way. Effectively, you can live however you want (good eh?).

The first question, therefore, is this......**how would you live your life?**

Let me expand – how would you spend your time? What things would you do? What would be your priorities now? Who would you spend your time with? What activities would give you the most fulfilment and allow you to live an enriched, meaningful life?

Finally, why did you give the answers you've just given? Why are those things important? How does it make you feel to just imagine the possibilities of it?

Before you move on to the next question spend 10-20 minutes on this. At this early stage of the book it's very easy to just skip over this to try and get to the money handling facts as quickly as possible but, if you do that, you're missing the point.

Going back to the journey analogy, it's the equivalent of jumping in your car and driving off without knowing where you're going. Yes, no doubt that by just getting in the car and driving you'll get somewhere, but when you look back towards the end of your journey, you run the risk of wishing you'd done much of it differently!

If you don't do this properly and you don't give it the time it deserves you'll never be able to 'marry your money to your meaning' so…..just stop a second.…..imagine the scenario I've given you….take it in…..and begin to imagine.

Once the vision of 'how you would live if money was no object 'starts to come to mind begin to **write down** your thoughts. In fact, if you're a creative person you can even draw your thoughts. By writing and drawing the images you have in your mind you start to program your subconscious mind into what you want it to achieve – and the subconscious mind has a big part to play in the process of goal setting.

Let me explain. In your brain there is something called the reticular activator. Its role is to act like a security guard on the doors of your brain and filter information in that you need and filter out information that you don't (think about it, if you noticed everything that you saw, smelt, felt, heard and touched your conscious brain would be overloaded and wouldn't be able to function).

To show you how this works have you ever bought a new car and then, once you've bought it, you start noticing lots of other people driving the same car? That's your reticular activator at work. Its bringing things to your attention that you've been focusing on.

So, when you start to set goals and create a plan for your life, if you write them down or draw them onto paper, you start to program your reticular activator as to what's important. It can then go to work for you by bringing things into your attention that will move you towards these goals and filtering out information that will have no benefit.

Another example is when a woman has a baby. She may have been a sound sleeper all her life but, when she has a baby, even the smallest sound from the baby can wake her up. That's because the reticular activator knows her baby is important and, guess what? Your reticular activator never sleeps! It's a 24 hour worker made especially for you. So why not use it?

For those of you that are interested in goal setting and how the brain works I can highly recommend the work Brian Mayne has done with his goal mapping process. Check him out online, he has some free templates you can use to develop your goals and understand the goal setting process further.

OK, hopefully you now understand how important it is to give the planning stage the time it needs. Now let's move on to the next question.

Question 2

You're sat in the doctor's. Your doctor is sat behind his desk looking at you with papers in his hand. He has the results of your test. He looks concerned. He alternates between looking at the report and glancing at you above his half rimmed glasses. Finally he speaks "I have some good news and some bad news. The good news is that you are going to have perfect health from now to the date of your death". He pauses, takes off his glasses and puts them on his desk and then looks directly at you. "The bad news is that you only have between 5 and 10 years to live."

What's become important to you now? Who has flashed into your mind? What are the things that will go to the top of your list and what will go to the bottom? What will go on your bucket list? What will you spend your time doing in the next 5 -10 years?

Again, take your time to imagine the scenario and answer as honestly as possible. Write/draw your answers down.

1. Question 3

Final scenario: Again, you're in the doctors. This time he looks even more concerned. "No good news this time I'm afraid" he says before dropping the bombshell "you only have 24 hours left to live". That's right; you have 24 hours to live!

The final question, therefore, is this – and it's not what are you going to do in the next 24 hours? Don't be rude!!! The question is *what do you wish **you would have done** in your life that you didn't?*

Tough one this isn't it? In fact it can be quite disturbing. The truth is this though, life is not a rehearsal.

So, again, imagine the scenario and then think about the question as if it's a real situation. Take your time and write down your answers.

These three questions, if answered with plenty of thought and some personal honesty, should reveal to you the things in life that are really important. Have a look at your answers. Is there a theme running through them; family, friends, loved ones, travel, maybe helping others? Worthwhile causes?

Whatever the answers are the main thing to ask you now is this-

Are you managing your finances in a manner that moves you closer to these goals and values or not?

This is a key point when we're attaching money to the 'happiness factor'. If your financial management is helping you achieve your ideal life then it's valid to say that money, in some way, can help to create happiness. If you're not, and you're like the majority of people who haven't established what's important to them, then money can be more of a problem than a blessing – regardless of how much or how little you have.

By 'marrying your money to your meaning' this can create a peace and a harmony that simply will not be achieved if your focus is simply on amassing more 'things' for the sake of it. If you feel that having more money will make you more acceptable then work on your self-image, not your bank balance.

Another major benefit of having a plan for your life is that it can give you a sense of purpose that you can focus your attention on. Having a goal that has a strong meaning or value to you will automatically make you narrow your attention and efforts towards actions that help you achieve it.

I'll give you an example of this. Dave, my business partner and certified financial planner decided to run a 10K race for charity (when I say race I really mean that some of the entrants were racing, not Dave you understand!). Now, once he set the goal and started collecting money guess what happened to his focus? That's right; he started thinking about how he was going to achieve it. Once he started thinking about it he started planning it and once he had planned it something else happened. He started running!

The funny thing is that he didn't even like running but, because his thoughts were leading his actions he started running. This action of 'doing something' made him progress towards his goal of finishing the race (notice I said finishing not racing).

Having a goal or a vision will automatically direct your efforts and habits towards the desired outcome and reduce your efforts away from things that move you away from your goals. Goals change your focus, your focus changes your habits and your habits change your results!

Another benefit of having a vision or goals written down is that it makes you more resistant to setbacks. If you are wandering around aimlessly, then any distraction or resistance can knock you off course. Having a goal helps you to stay on track when things get tough – and believe me, any goal that is worthwhile will come with some form of challenge or sacrifice, that's one surety.

OK, I'm now assuming that you have a clear vision of the things in life that are important and you've started to learn that financial planning is not about your money; it's about your life. In fact, as the book cover say's it's about getting the best life you can with the money you've got. Now let's move onto the second stage in the initial planning process.

2. Creating your lifeline.

Once you have your values and ideals in place we can move onto what I call 'creating your *lifeline*'.

Your *lifeline* is an imaginary line that starts at your current age and continues until the sobering thought of a realistic age of death. Now I know that no-one knows how old we will be when we die (though I have included a mortality table below to give you a sobering idea) but I would suggest that you keep things optimistic. After all, you don't want to run out of money too long before you run out of life!

Below is a life expectancy table at birth and at age 65 for the UK and constituent countries for 2008-2010.

	At birth		At age 65	
	Males	**Females**	**Males**	**Females**
United Kingdom	78.1	82.1	17.8	20.4
England	78.4	82.4	18.0	20.6
Wales	77.5	81.7	17.5	20.1
Scotland	75.8	80.3	16.6	19.2
Northern Ireland	77.0	81.4	17.3	20.1

Table source: Office for National Statistics

As you can see a male born in between 2008-2010 will live, on average, 78.1 years and woman will live 82.1 years. If you reached the age of 65 in the same years then a man can expect, on average, to live a further 17.8 years (and reach almost 83) and a woman can expect another 20.4 years to take her past 85. Sobering thought eh?

If I'm creating a financial plan for someone I will usually use the age of 90 for over 50 year olds and 100 for under 40 year olds, with a discussion for those aged between. If you think that's too optimistic then have a look at the stats now for how longevity is increasing. Paternoster, a final salary scheme buyout specialist, has done a study which suggested that half of 30 year olds can expect to live to age 100. In fact the fastest growing age group in the industrialized world is the centenarian club. That's right, those living past the age of 100 are the fastest growing age range.

Most demographic studies agree that in 20 years from now there will be about a million of us enjoying the three digit lifestyle. Oh, and those studies don't even count on the revolutionary longevity treatments we could develop in the next 20 years.

It may also be sensible to take into account any health issues too when considering your longevity. As I write this I'm 44 years of age and actuarial table's state I will live to 84.5! That means I'm just over half way through my life. What a great time to look at all I've learned, good and bad, and put into practice all the good, ditch the bad and focus on having a great future.

So, the start of your *lifeline* is your current age and the end of your *lifeline* is your predicted mortality - plus a few years.

If you are 30 therefore it should now look as complicated as this-

30 35 40 45 50 55 60 65 70 75 80 85 90 95 100

Is that a bit easier than working out the angles of a dodecahedron?
Now let's move onto the next part in the process.

3. Recognising and deciding on your life stages and events.

Once you have your answers from the lifestyle questions above together with your *lifeline* we can now move onto the next stage where you can start thinking about *life events* or *life stages* that you want to plan for. These items are a little less 'spiritual' than the questions asked above.

To explain-

A life event is a **one off** transaction that will need a financial commitment.

A life stage is a **period of time** that requires a financial commitment.

A life event is a one off transaction that will need a financial commitment. A life stage is a period of time that requires a financial commitment.

For example, a life event may be a house move, a daughter's wedding or a world cruise; something that's a one off.

A life stage may be university education for children, retirement or looking after elderly parents.

They're stages rather than events purely because the cost of them will impact over several years rather than being a one time expense.

In essence your *lifeline*, once you've added your life events and stages to it, is a bit like a chronological bucket list – a list of things you want to do before you die.

By the way if you've not seen the film 'The Bucket List' with Morgan Freeman and Jack Nicholson then I urge you to watch it. It's a great way to explain the 'things to do before I die' issue.

The items that you add to your *lifeline* will obviously be unique however, to assist you, I've given a list of both events and stages that occur regularly in conversations I have with clients.

Please note that this, in no way, is an exhaustive list. It's just an aid to get you thinking what type of life events or stages that you may want to achieve or prepare for.

What is important is that ***you create your own list***, a list of events that YOU want to achieve, a list of stages that YOU want to provide for, basically a list of things that are important to YOU.

This can take a bit of time but it can lead to some great discussions if you do it properly. Also, try to ensure that your life stages or life events are in sync with the answers you gave to the 3 value's based questions above. If not, you won't create the right balance in your time versus money quest.

Another benefit of identifying the events and stages is that it leads back to what I was saying earlier about goals. When you have the important things in your life written down it helps you to start managing your finances in a way that leads you towards these goals. If your *lifeline* is visible then it helps the important things to stick in your mind so, when you're faced with a choice about whether you should spend a fortune on something you've just seen advertised on TV, you can go back to your *lifeline* and either add it to it or decide if it's not a priority. Anyway, here are some suggestions to get you thinking but please, create your own. It's your life after all.

Life Events	Life Stages
Deposit for home	Provide for young families
Annual holidays	Build/furnish family home
40th birthday	Kids University Education
Regular car purchase	Start a new business
50th birthday	Start to reduce debt
Pay off mortgage	Semi- Retirement
2nd home?	Empty nesting phase
World Cruise	World travel
Ensure family estate protected	Full retirement
Downsize	Care, healthcare costs
Amend property	Charity, family, home Comforts
Special weddings/anniversaries	

NOW WRITE SOME OF YOUR OWN BELOW

When we come to the next step in the planning process you will be able to have a visible image of your life goals in front of you. This is a powerful image to have and one that really focuses the mind on how to achieve it.

4. Place your chosen events and stages onto your lifeline

If you look at the list of potential events and stages I've just given you, you will notice that they've been placed in age related order i.e. a deposit for a home and providing for young families comes before paying off your mortgage or full retirement. The reason for this is that it makes sense to add your items on to the *lifeline* in chronological order. That way, when you look visually at your *timeline* it becomes easy to understand as it relates to how you will progress through your life. It literally becomes a visual map of your journey with each life stage or life event becoming a pit stop.

Each pit stop is effectively an opportunity to get out the car, stretch your legs, enjoy the moment along the way and celebrate your achievement.

After all, we have to remember that this is a journey and happiness will come from enjoying the whole journey, not just the final destination.

So, an example *lifeline* for a 45 year old might look something like this –

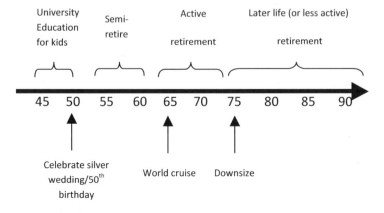

As you can see, in this example, the life stages have been placed on the top of the *lifeline* and the life events have been placed under the *lifeline*. This is simply to make it easier to view.

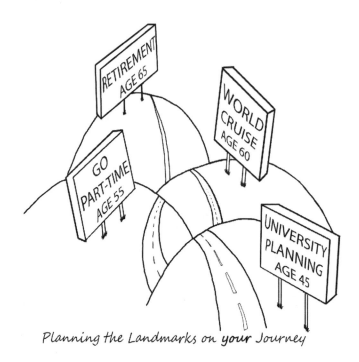

Planning the Landmarks on your Journey

Once you've done YOUR *lifeline* you should now be starting to build a visible picture of your ideal future.

I'm not saying here that you should be unrealistic by the way. This isn't necessarily a positive thinking book. It's more a workshop of how to get the best out of what you've got. It's more practical than motivational. However, I would suggest that you don't limit yourself and be too cautious as we'll cover prioritising in a short while.

As mentioned already, my aim for writing this book is to give you a process where you read, do and apply. Those of you who follow the processes in each chapter, I promise it will have a major impact on the quality of your financial life. For those of you that don't then, at best this book will just be an interesting read.

Ok, my suggestion is that you now spend some time creating and working on YOUR *lifeline*. Make that chronological bucket list of yours with the life events and stages that you want to plan for, starting at your current age and ending at a realistic age of death. Once you've done it (and only when you've done it) we can successfully move onto the next step in creating your financial plan.

5. Work out the costs

Apart from discussing your life events and life stages this is the only other stage that might take a little work and a little research (so this is the point where we might lose some of you that haven't really identified the importance of your goals).

The big dreamers amongst you will have a bigger challenge here as you may look at the list of events and stages on your *lifeline* and think 'there's no way I/we can afford to do all that'.

Well you know what? You're probably right but, even if you do have big ambitions isn't it better to try and fail than never to try at all?

It's like the sat nav analogy I gave you earlier, simply by using one you will have a much greater chance of getting to your destination quicker and with less fuel costs than trying to 'play it by ear'.

Having a plan and managing your finances with a purpose will almost certainly enable you to tick more of those goals off your *lifeline* than not having one. I would guarantee this by the way but, being regulated by the FSA for so many years has moulded me into a person that isn't allowed to say 'guarantee' for anything – saying 'almost certainly' is a big deal for me!.

Ok, so how do we work out the costs? Well you could start by doing a bit of research. Want a world cruise at 65? Then go on the internet, type in world cruise and find out how much they cost today.

Actually the curiosity just got the better of me there so I did it myself. You're looking at £7-10000 per person with what I saw in a very brief browse.

OK, you now have the cost (gulp) what you need to do now is add some inflation to the price because, if you're 35 now they won't be £7-10,000 in 30 years time! Just like a mars bar wasn't 60 pence 30 years ago. In fact, if my memory serves me right, Mr Rudkin used to sell them for 7pence in the top shop when I was a kid.

So, to create a realistic cost of a world cruise in 30 years time we need to understand a simple way to factor in inflation to the plan. Let's begin by assuming it will be 4% per annum for the next 30 years. This means that a £7000 cruise today will really cost around £22,700 in 30 years time. Adding inflation into the cost is fairly easy. You can do it on a calculator by putting £7000 into a calculator and then pressing + 4% 30 times or simply go on the internet and search for compound interest tables. There's quite a few on different websites you can use without cost.

So, once you've added inflation to the initial costs add that figure to the life event on your *lifeline* like this-

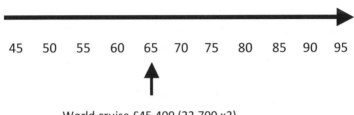

World cruise £45,400 (22,700 x2)

Now, all you need to do is to continue doing this for the rest of the life events on your *lifeline*. This may take a little time but it is fun. In fact it can be really exciting to dream and plan. Remember what I said about the psychological effect of setting goals? Well you can literally start to see it develop as you start to piece the jigsaw puzzle of your 'life-plan' together.

Once you've done this we'll do something similar for the life stages but, in the meantime, put the book down and start to 'do' rather than 'read'.

Hey, you're back. Great stuff!

OK, I really hope you've started to take action by now. Believe me, just thinking about it is as much use as 'just thinking about driving somewhere', in reality you're going nowhere until you take action and decide where you're going, motivate yourself to get off your backside and pick up the car keys!

Let's move on now onto how to plan and cost for the life events. Remember, life events are where the impact will be over a longer time frame. This is slightly different in that you have to take into account the length of time of the event together with the cost. This impact could be an extra expenditure (like university education for kids) or reduced income (like retirement) or even both.

The basics still remain the same, in that you need to research the costs for the extra expenditure, factor in inflation and then factor in the number of years. However, what can often be more difficult is factoring in a reduction of income, say in retirement or semi-retirement. This is where (again) you have to imagine yourself into the future as if it were happening today.

Let's look at retiring for example. We will cover this in more detail in chapter 9 but, essentially, what you have to do here is forecast what the potential loss of income will be together with the expenditure requirements.

So, if you earn £30,000 today and your pension forecast says you will retire on half of this then you know that your future income, in today's terms, will be £15,000. The challenge now is to work out what your expenditure will be to see if the £15,000 is enough.

Now don't get too concerned thinking that this is too complicated. I have devoted a full chapter to budgeting as well as a full chapter to 'retiring without losing your lifestyle' so there's plenty of information for you to get an understanding of this later in the book.

In essence, all we are trying to establish is what the extra annual cost OR the annual decrease in income will be, and then place this on your *lifeline* where the life stages are.

Here's an example from the previous *lifeline* of a 45 year old, now with the life stages added on –

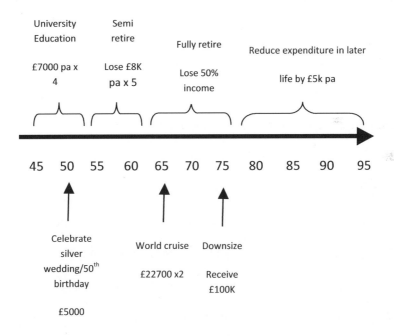

Hopefully, once you've done this, you will start to have a pretty good (and easy to understand) plan of what you want to achieve and what will be required to achieve it. Your plan should now be coming together as your lifeline is now pretty much complete. You can see some of the events and life stages and the anticipation of the costs.

Also, if you're really observant, you will have noticed on the last *lifeline* that we now have something which shows an amount of income coming into the household in the 'downsize' item. This imaginary client has obviously worked out that he/she is willing to sell their property and buy something £100,000 cheaper.

So, this now leads on to the next step of 'adding in any likely receipts'.

6. Add in likely receipts

We've mentioned downsizing above. What other areas could you include here? How about maturities from savings plans? Tax free lump sums from retirement, inheritances, sale of assets etc?

Placing these items on to your *lifeline* are just as valid as placing the likely expenses on there as they will have an impact on your life time cash flow.

For example, we have identified that, if a world cruise is a priority on your *lifeline* then you need to have £45,000 available at that time (no, don't think about borrowing it – you will see why in chapter 5, Ditch the Debt).

So, if you can identify that your company or private pensions are forecasting a tax free lump sum of around that same figure, then hey presto, life event no.2 (the world cruise), sorted!

This means you don't have to plan for it like you might have to for the other items, it's already covered.

In fact, by looking at what is needed and then adding in what is already in place you are then just left with the list of things that you still need to prepare for.

So, the penultimate stage in the planning process is adding in any likely receipts.

The difficult one here is always the 'inheritance' issue. I would generally like to err on the cautious side here and suggest you attempt to achieve the majority of your events/stages without relying on

Don't forget to place anticipated receipts onto your lifeline just as you have done with anticipated expenditure.

this. If your parents live to 120 you might regret it or, even worse, if their health deteriorates and the local authority decides to seize their assets to pay for their care costs then it can be painful seeing your parents become ill AND have all their assets erode away. This is happening to over 40,000 families per year in the UK and will only increase as we live for longer.

Besides, how do you know that your parents are going to leave you anything anyway? I say let them enjoy their money, let them get the best life they can with what they've got and concentrate on their love and memories rather than their parting financial gifts. (Hmmm, awkward subject isn't it?). Anyway, moving on!

Once you've added all your events and life stages on to your *lifeline* and you've factored in the anticipated costs/likely receipts you should then 'see' a vision of your intended financial future. **A future that is infinitely more likely to happen now that you've started to write it down and plan for it.**

By having a vision like this all on one page you should also get an idea of which events and stages are going to cause you trouble i.e. which ones are going to be most costly!

You should also know which of your goals are the most important and therefore your assets/disposable income should be moved towards that item as a priority. If you can see that, in 10 years, your kids will need their university costs to be funded and you haven't allocated anything towards it then you know you have some work to do.

However, if there are other items on your *lifeline* that are more important to you then you may want to put the university education costs in the '**would like to**' box rather than the '**have to**' box.

So this is where we move onto the last stage in the initial planning process, the prioritisation process.

7. Prioritise

If you are looking at your *lifeline* and thinking 'that's no problem to achieve all of that' then you are either wealthy already or have very inexpensive desires.

Now there's nothing wrong with either of them if it fits in with the first thing i.e. evaluating what's really important to you. However, if you've placed lots of events and stages on your *lifeline* then achieving **everything** is most likely to be a challenge. In fact, for some of you it will be an achievement if you manage to accomplish half of them but, as I said earlier, don't worry about it. I don't know anyone who has achieved absolutely everything they wanted (although that's partly because I don't have any oil sheiks as clients).

I suppose it's a half full not half empty philosophy really but I know that you achieve far more by having your goals written down as *"The key is to set your goals high and take pleasure in ticking them off one by one rather than being upset about the ones you didn't achieve".* opposed to just thinking about it. However, there is something we can do today to make sure the important ones are achieved – and that's to prioritise.

OK, to help you with your prioritising, here's another one of those 'imagining scenarios' for you –

Look at your life stages and life events that you've placed on your *lifeline*. Imagine that you have the same number of blank post it notes as the number of events and stages you have put down.

Now imagine there are 2 ballot boxes in front of you with the words '**Have To**' and '**Would Like To**' on each one separately. Write down each of your individual goals on their own post it note and then place each one either in the 'Have To' box or the 'Would Like To' box.

The 'have to' box represents the items that you NEED to plan for (let's say retirement) whereas the 'would like to' box represents items that would be nice but won't really cause you a problem if you don't achieve them (for example the world cruise). A 'have to' isn't always a 'would like to' either. It's more a 'if I don't do it I'm in trouble' scenario!

Another way of prioritising is to look at the list of items and then simply put them in order of desire.

If you're not sure which items are the most important then look at the life stage/event and ask yourself 'if I don't accomplish this will it cause me a real problem or will it just cause me some disappointment?'

If it will cause you a problem then it's a priority, if it will just cause disappointment then it's a 'would like to' item. Priorities, or the 'have to', should always be planned for first, followed by the most important 'would like to' afterwards.

For example, you might really enjoy a 6 month world cruise at 65 but if you have nothing left for the next 20-30 years of your retirement you'll have a problem that will soon make you forget how much you enjoyed it!

Hopefully, you will now have your plan taking shape. Don't worry if you feel like you've missed things or not calculated things to the penny. Financial planning should never be a one off event anyway. Instead, it's a constantly evolving program of planning, doing, monitoring and adjusting and you should return to it regularly.

When an airline pilot flies a plane or a captain sails a ship they will factor into their journey all the major and minor details. Yes they will know the destination, the anticipated time of arrival, the number of people they will be carrying and the amount of fuel they will need but did you know that most of the time they will be going off course – even with the sophisticated auto pilot systems they have these days. That's because they can't fully take into account every situation, like Mother Nature for instance.

The winds will always be moving the plane nearer or further away from its path, the tides will always be trying to move the ship off course. They know this and that's why they're constantly tinkering with the controls; a small degree here, a little change there – constantly working to stay on track when lots of things are trying to get them off course.

Readers, that's life I'm afraid. The only thing I will promise in this book is that life will change along the way. Your plans may even be altered significantly, but, by having a plan, you will be prepared for most outcomes and you should be able to stay on track when 'mother nature' tries to put you off course too.

So go on, finish your *lifeline*. If you don't you won't get the benefit and, since this is a book on making the most of your finances, don't waste the money you've spent to buy it without getting the full benefit!

OK, we're now at the end of the initial planning process so let's recap.

1. **Evaluate what's important** - Working on the assumption that money, in itself, will not make you happy always remember that aligning your money with your meaning will create far more peace of mind and happiness than just amassing 'things.'

2. **Create your lifeline** - Being able to see a map or a plan of your long term future is akin to getting out a map or a sat-nav and looking at the whole of your journey in one place. It helps you to 'see your future' and what potential traffic jams or landmarks you will want or need to prepare for.

3. **Decide on the life events or life stages** - Your life events or stages, as mentioned above, are the landmarks or potential problems you want and need to plan/prepare for on your journey. Be they events that require a one off expense or a life stage that will require a longer financial commitment, having them placed on your lifeline helps you to maximise the chance of enjoying the journey.

4. **Place them on your lifeline** - By putting them on your lifeline in chronological order you can see where on your journey they will be. This helps you to factor in the time you have to plan and prepare for

them.

5. **Calculate the costs** - By adding in the anticipated costs your 'journey' you now have the practical aspect of having to prepare financially. If you know what the cost will be you can start to allocate resources accordingly.

6. **Add in Likely Receipts** - Life will sometimes give you something as well as take away from you – especially if you've given or sacrificed in the first place. Factoring in the anticipated sums of money you are likely to receive from the various sources will help you to see how many of your landmarks are already provided for and thus how many are not. It's like comparing the fuel you already have in your tank to the amount needed to get where you want to go.

7. **Prioritise** - Dream big so you will have an incentive. However, be aware that only the very wealthy or those that require very little from life will probably achieve everything. Be sensible, therefore, and prioritise the items that you feel are most important. Use the 'have to' or 'would like to' filter to help you.

Now onto chapter 2....Budgeting

Chapter 2 – Establish your Budget

Annual income twenty pounds, annual expenditure nineteen and six,
result happiness.

Annual income twenty pounds, annual expenditure twenty pounds ought
and six, result misery.

~David Copperfield, Charles Dickens

Once you have your *lifeline* completed you now have an image of your desired journey. What we need to do next is to organise your finances to give you the best chance of achieving this journey. To do this it's important that you're organised and prepared.

This chapter, therefore, deals with budgeting. By the way did you know that the word budget originates from the French word, *bougette*, which means purse in

"It's not what you earn that counts, it's what you keep."

English? There you go, two snippets of culture for you in the very first page of this chapter, Dickens and French!

Here's a statement worth remembering– **it's only what you keep that can be allocated towards your life events and life stages.** Budgeting, therefore, forces us to get organised and manage our finances with both a short and long term view. A good financial plan should enable you to do all the things you want to do today *and* tomorrow, without running out of money.

Paul Armson, a successful adviser and promoter of 'lifestyle financial planning' uses a diagram to explain the concept of enjoying life today and tomorrow. He explains it like this-

'Assume you have a bucket. Inside the bucket are all the things you can use *today* as cash in order to exchange for your chosen lifestyle. This will include your bank/building society accounts, endowment policies, investments, shares etc. In other words, anything you can get your hands on within a week or two to spend.

Outside of your bucket are other assets that you may own such as your property, your pension funds, the value of your business etc. Now, I'm not saying that these aren't assets but we can't include them IN your bucket until you sell them or reach the age you can collect them. I mean, you can't chip a few bricks off your house and take them to Tesco's as a trade for your groceries can you?

You also have a flow of income coming into your bucket. This will be from salaries, benefits, interest earned, rental income, dividends etc. These will be filling up your bucket and providing the resources for you to live your life today. The bad news is that this flow of income will vary. Sometimes it will be high when your career is at its peak but sometimes it will be more of a trickle, say when you are young, made redundant or if you haven't prepared for your retirement years sufficiently.

Some more bad news is that the bucket has a tap at the bottom. I say tap rather than hole as a tap can be opened as wide as you need in order to

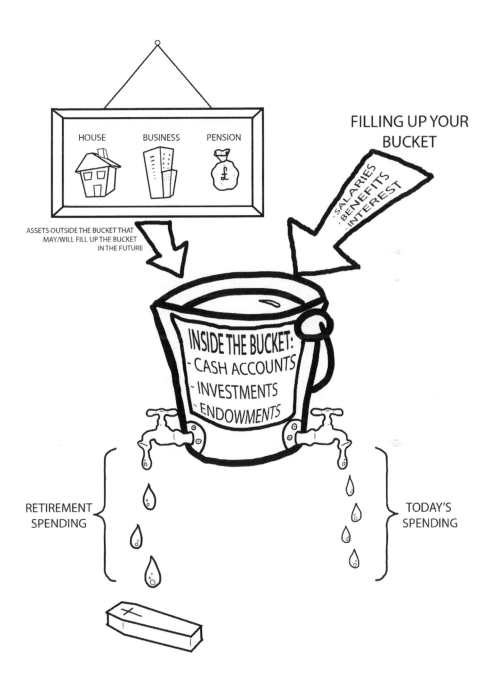

FILLING UP YOUR BUCKET

HOUSE   BUSINESS   PENSION

- SALARIES
- BENEFITS
- INTEREST

ASSETS OUTSIDE THE BUCKET THAT
MAY/WILL FILL UP THE BUCKET
IN THE FUTURE

INSIDE THE BUCKET:
- CASH ACCOUNTS
- INVESTMENTS
- ENDOWMENTS

RETIREMENT
SPENDING

TODAY'S
SPENDING

provide 'enough' for you to live today. It can also be tightened to stem the flow and even turned off all together. This tap is usually dripping money out of the bucket like you wouldn't believe. It's this tap that provides money for the mortgage, the kids, the holidays, the supermarket shopping, the private yacht expenses (oh come on we all have one don't we?)

However, there will come a time when this 'income tap' is turned off and the flow of the income into the bucket stops. This will then mean the 'expenditure tap' will probably need to be replaced by a 'retirement tap' – one that is turned on a little less fully. And that's the rub. Why, if you've had the 'income tap' running for 40 years do many people find that there's not enough in the bucket to last for the rest of your life?

Simple, if you haven't assessed your lifestyle needs both before and after your working life, and then allocated your resources towards them it's highly likely you won't have enough and something will have to be sacrificed.

The secret to financial planning, therefore, is to be able to achieve all your goals without compromising your value's, both today AND tomorrow – without the fear of the bucket ever running out of money.'

The perfect scenario would be to reach the end of your life, having achieved all the things you want to do, with £1 left in your French *bougette* (OK, I'm not including any amounts to leave for your loved ones to inherit in this example but you get the point I'm sure).

However, whilst I'm on this subject, leaving a mortgage free property to loved ones is always a noble and commendable achievement.

So what are the reasons for establishing your budget?

Contrary to popular opinion a budget does not have to deprive you of the good life. A budget is there simply to help keep you on the right track.

It is also the cornerstone of building wealth. In the book 'The Millionaire Next Door' by TJ Stanley & WD Danko they studied how the majority of America's millionaires

Budgeting doesn't have to rob you of the good life today. It's there simply to keep you on track.

became wealthy. They found that the majority of the people who achieved the millionaire status came from normal backgrounds. In other words they didn't inherit it or achieve it through being gifted at some sport or other. They did it by creating 'an artificial environment of scarcity.' This then enabled them to save far more money for their futures than their counterparts. This is what you call a 'pay yourself first mentality' and it's this that helped them achieve their wealth.

So how do you budget?

Your budget starts with calculating the net income (income received after tax) that comes into your household (or bucket). Don't forget to make sure you include ALL sources of income such as salary, bonus, allowances, benefits etc. If your income is variable then try and establish an average that you feel comfortable using, maybe based on an average over the preceding year. If you receive bonuses on an annual basis then this is ideal to put to one side and use for your goals (as long as you're not living beyond your means and then having to use it to clear off annual overdrafts etc). Basically, get to a point where you can put down the most accurate figure for what income comes into your household each month.

Whilst we're on this subject please ensure you are receiving all the income you are entitled to. Earlier this year, HM Revenue & Customs revealed that around £5billion of working tax credit and child tax credit goes unclaimed annually, bringing the total of money that fails to reach those in need to 13billion pounds! Your local council, HMRC and organisations such as the citizen's advice bureau should be able to help you here. Also, if you are self-employed, speak to your accountant to make sure that all legitimate business expenses are being claimed for.

Once you have your monthly net income the next thing to do is **list your expenditure.**

An important element here is that you **use your bank account statements to analyse this.** Yes it's easy to remember items like gas, electric, mortgage costs etc but it's also very easy to forget ad-hoc purchases or underestimate the amount you spend on general items such as the quick trip to the DIY store or the family trip to the cinema etc

A good way of establishing how accurate your expenditure list is this... if your net household income is £2000 and your expenditure is £1500 then where is the spare £500 from last month? If you can identify it then what about the £6000 you have acquired over the year? If you can genuinely see your bank account or net worth increasing like this then your expenditure is probably correct. If, like many, you can't put your hands immediately on the saved money then re-check your expenditure as you're probably forgetting or underestimating things.

So let's have a look at the benefits of establishing your budget.

1. It helps you to establish your disposable income

As mentioned earlier your disposable income is the amount of money that you have left over after all your expenses and needs have been met. The purpose of establishing your disposable income is that it is this money that can be allocated towards your future life stages and events. It's also this disposable income that you can use to protect against your concerns and maintain your lifestyle in the future.

By establishing your disposable income and then earmarking it towards your goals and value's you have a better chance of creating a memory. In other words it helps you to align your money with your meaning and create more joy and value in your life.

The problem I find, however, is that budgeting does not come naturally to everyone. What I find regularly (if not always) is that, if a client has disposable income but is not allocating it to a life event or life stage then most of it will probably just filter through their fingers. That's because budgeting is a habit that requires discipline.

There are many internet sites these days that can provide you with a free expenditure form. We have one on our website that automatically calculates your disposable income for you. It will also calculate where your money is going and then gives you a pie chart of your expenditure. This can be found on the link page of our website at www.idealfinancialmanagement.co.uk

There are also an increasing number of websites and Apps that are becoming available to help you monitor your expenditure these days. These tools often link in to your online banking facilities so they can accurately track your expenditure, producing graphs and images of where your money is going.

I'd recommend you have a look at these and find one that's suitable. Your bank may even have one for you.

2. It helps you to 'find the leaks'

Once you have created your budget the next step is to analyse where your money is going and where potential savings can be made. In other words – find the leaks in your bucket!

Let's face it, we all waste money. From not shopping around for the best deals or simply throwing food away every week that you bought but haven't eaten. If you really think about it we must collectively waste millions of pounds per year. Yet it's this money we could be using to help us achieve our goals. In fact, without having any disposable income the chapters around saving, investing and planning for retirement are all pretty pointless if you don't have any money to allocate to these goals.

So, I just want to give out a few money saving tips if that's OK? I don't intend to produce a massive list but I do want to focus on a few key areas where people normally spend (and therefore often waste) a lot of their earned income.

So here we go with a few ideas…..as my mother always used to say "if you look after the pennies, the pounds will look after themselves".

Firstly, once you've created your expenditure ask yourself the following 3 questions:-

a) do I need it

b) is it moving me towards my goals

c) can I reduce the cost?

For example, let's say you spend £100 per week on your supermarket shopping. The first question 'do I need it' is obviously yes as it's fair to say that food is an essential item. The second question 'Is it moving me towards your goals is also yes – it's keeping you alive! The third question 'can I reduce the cost' is also probably yes.

> *"Do I need it, is it moving me towards my goals and can I reduce the cost"?*

So how could you reduce the cost here? Well this is where you could review the waste as mentioned above. Maybe you could use your local market instead of the supermarket? Maybe organise your shopping so that you're not buying food for evenings that you've organised to eat out? Shop online so you only buy the essentials and don't get tempted by the end of shelf 'bargains' that you don't really need?

By making small changes like this you could probably manage to reduce your weekly bill from £100 to £80 per week.

Now I know that doesn't sound a lot but when you work it out, a saving of £20 per week is actually £1040 per annum. What can you do with £1040 per year that WOULD make a difference? Move from a 3 star to a 5 star annual family holiday? Pay the car loan off 12 months earlier? Invest it to retire earlier?

Did you know that if you saved £20 per week from age 30 and stop at age 60 you will have **£105,723** assuming a return of 7% per year? Starts to add up over time doesn't it?

What about other ways to 'find the leaks'?

Have you ever shopped around on your car insurance and saved a £100? What about finding that Christmas present £20 cheaper online than in the local shop? The internet now is a massive tool that people can use to save money. You can even download free apps on your smart phones now that allow you to scan bar codes in to see where you can buy the product cheaper!

Another example is using vouchers. A couple of months ago we decided to go to Alton Towers. Now I could've gone down to Alton Towers, joined the queue and paid around £100 for 2 adults and 2 kids to enter the park. However, just as a fleeting thought the day prior I decided to type 'Alton towers discounts' into Google and about 2 minutes later I was printing off a half price voucher for a family of four, giving me a saving of £50 for 2 minutes work. That's better than a solicitor's hourly rate!

On the other side of the coin have you ever been into the supermarket for a loaf of bread and then come out half an hour later with £25 of goods?

Another suggestion is to make sure you have a competitive mortgage rate. If you are paying the variable rate with your lender it's highly likely they will have a better rate for you (if you ask them) or another lender will allow you to transfer your debt and benefit from a lower interest payment.

Here's a quick question, how much wasted food goes in your bin each week? According to the 'Love food, hate waste' campaign Britons wasted around 6.7 billion tons of food in 2007. This is food that's been bought, paid for and carried home…but not eaten. In the USA statistics from the National Institute of Diabetes and Digestive and Kidney Diseases show that 40% of food goes to waste. Proof that being organised with your shopping can save you £000's throughout the year.

Not shopping around for your utility bills, your household bills and your insurances can also be a big source of wasted cash. Make sure you review these annually to make sure the cover is appropriate and you get the most competitive premiums.

Shop around and negotiate on large purchases. It's not a crime to ask for a discount and, in many cases, you will be adequately rewarded? In the UK we seem to think that you only negotiate when buying a car or a house but you can (and probably will) save 000's when you apply this to other major purchases. Ask if the seller does price matching or pose the simple question 'what's the minimum you will take for your product?'

Make sure you don't have standing orders or direct debits going out without knowing what they're for. I regularly meet clients who, when analysing their bank statements for what is probably the first time, they see outgoings for items that they have no idea what they're actually for. I've seen people with 3 separate policies for building insurance yet they only have one house!

Watch your TV package. Many people pay expensive monthly contracts for channels they never watch.

Keep an eye on your travel costs. Let's face it, petrol isn't cheap at the moment and driving more miles than you need to can soon notch up the fuel bill. Rather than dropping a document off with someone can you just email it instead? Can you car share with a work colleague? Not only are you saving money but you're reducing your carbon footprint at the same time.

One final way to look at the lost value in spending money where it's not necessary is this-

You understand that you buy goods with money you've earned by sacrificing your time right? So what do you think is more valuable, time or money?

Well personally I think time is more valuable than money because, if you lose money you can get it back but if you lose time, forget it, it's gone and it will never come back. So if you're net income is £10 per hour and you waste £40 per week by being unorganised then essentially you're working one morning per week for

If you're net income is £10 per hour and you waste £40 per week by being unorganised then essentially you're working one morning per week for nothing

nothing. You may as well stay in bed. It's worthless. And if time is worth more than money then why are you trading 4 valuable hours of your life for a commodity of less value?

Now please don't misunderstand me. I'm not asking you to sell your home, sleep in a tent and live off the land. All I'm saying is this – spend some time analysing your expenditure and make sure that you maximise what comes in and make sure what goes out is of value. If it IS of value make sure you're not overpaying for it, if it's NOT of value then dump it or minimise it.

3. It helps you to focus and prioritise.

A route of many roads leading from nowhere to nothing.
~Ambrose Bierce

Once you have created your budget, maximised your income and then looked at ways of avoiding wasted expenditure you then have the disposable income that is available as mentioned above. **The key to good budgeting is**

to get your disposable income as high as possible without reducing your lifestyle today.

This is where the prioritising comes in so you can allocate the correct amount to each goal and put the money in the most suitable account (or tax wrapper) so that the right amount is available at the right time whilst maximising returns.

By aligning your expenditure in a way that moves you towards your goals rather than away from them is one of the secrets to maximising your money.

This is where you can start to see the potential turnaround in your financial position and you can start to understand how the goals on your *lifeline* can become achievable. That's because now you will be starting to focus on achieving specific results rather than having no plan for your life or your money. This is the foundation that the saving and investing chapters are built on. These can be learnt in chapters 7 & 8.

Once you've arrived at a monthly disposable income figure go back to your *lifeline* and see which items on your list you can start allocating the funds to. Start with the highest priority first and then work down until they're all covered or, what's more likely, you run out of money.

For example, let's say you've analysed there is £500 per month disposable income now. I would envisage that there's probably scope to find another £200 by being organised and shopping

The key to good budgeting is to get your disposable income as high as possible without reducing your lifestyle today.

around. So that means you now have £700 to allocate towards your life events and life stages. If you look at *your lifeline* you can start to see how that can be allocated towards the highest priority in the 'have to's' list, then start allocating what's spare to the next item on the list and so on.

I must admit that this is where the skills of a good financial planner will help you together with the tools and software they have that make the calculations easier. However, as this is aimed at helping you do your own planning, you will probably be able to get most of it done with some time, patience and a calculator.

4. It helps you to stay organised.

Organising your budget is good. Keeping on top of it and staying organised is even better. Remember budgeting is a habit and habits need to be formed by discipline. It may not be the most exciting part of your month but spending 15-20 minutes just analysing where your money has gone that month and looking at what's left (if any) will fine tune your focus on where to spend your hard earned cash. The exciting bit is when you start to find that you're now running out of month before you run out of money and can put even more spare cash away towards your goals.

So, that's about it for chapter 2 – Organising your Budget. You're probably thinking that in the next chapter we'll be moving onto where to put your savings to make them work for you but that's not the case.

After all, you've now planned your journey. You've fuelled up. What we need to do next before we set off is make sure you know where you're starting from.

Finally here's a summary of chapter 2 - The Importance of Establishing a Budget

1. Establish your net household income and make sure you are receiving all your entitlements

2. Go through your bank statements to provide an accurate list of your expenditure

3. Analyse your expenditure to see where savings can be made.

4. Establish your disposable income and allocate it towards your needs.

5. Prioritise and focus these savings

6. Stay organised by checking your expenditure regularly.

Now onto chapter 3…Know what you're worth

Chapter 3 – Know what you're worth

"The quickest way to double your money is to fold it in half and put it in your back pocket."

~Will Rogers

One of the best ways to check your overall progress in financial planning terms is to create a net worth statement. Doing this early on in the financial planning process is a great marker for

"Your net worth is simply this – a table of your assets minus your liabilities".

the journey. It's like putting your milometer to zero before you set off and turning on your sat nav so it can identify where you are now, where you want to go and how far you need to travel.

In essence a net worth statement is simply a table of your assets minus your liabilities but, when analysed, it can be a great tool for your long term financial success.

Why create a net worth statement?

There are many benefits of a net worth statement:-

- It gives you a bird's eye view of the overall state of your finances.
- It allows you to see how close you are to your goals (especially the goal of financial freedom)

- You can analyse which assets are working for you and which are working against you
- You can see whether you are over or under exposed to certain areas
- It provides a monitoring tool to check your progress.

A net worth statement shows you the resources you have to work with. I suppose it's a bit like creating a mind map of your finances where you can see all the important points on one sheet.

We will cover the above point in more detail later in this chapter, but first, let's look at how to create a net worth statement.

How to create a net worth statement

The first thing I suggest you do is make a list of your assets and allocate them into different sectors such as -

liquid assets, investments, pension funds, properties, cars, valuables, furnishings, other e.g. value of business.

If you are married then it will be a good idea to create a separate column for each partner, a joint column and a total column. Once you've done this you can then start adding up all your liabilities and take these values away from your assets to create your net worth. Your liabilities may include items such as –

mortgages, loans, overdrafts, hire purchase items, visas, store cards as well as any other personal debts to family etc

Table 1 on the next page gives you an example of how this may look for an example client, Mark & Julie.

Once you have arrived at your net worth figure put the current date on it. This signals the start of your journey so, in the future, you can monitor the progress.

As mentioned earlier a benefit of creating a net worth statement is that it allows you to see which assets are moving you towards your goal and which are moving you away.

We can see an example of this in Table 2. All items in grey are creating an income and/or capital growth (and therefore moving Mark & Julie towards their goals) and all items in GREY CAPITALS are reducing their capital or disposable income (and so moving them away from their goals).

By coding (or differentiating) assets and liabilities we start to get a picture of what they have working for them and what they have working against them.

I know it's simple but the idea is obviously to build up the assets and reduce the liabilities so that, over time, it's possible to achieve financial freedom. So when you have this bird's eye view it then reveals how close you are to your goals and what you can do to get there.

Now let's use this net worth chart as an example on how you can use it to create financial freedom. Financial freedom by the way is effectively having an income that covers your expenditure without having to do something you don't want to do in order to get it.

TABLE 1	Mark	Julie	Joint	TOTAL
Liquid Assets				
Bank Accounts	900	800	400	2100
Cash ISA's	3000	4200		7200
Stocks & Shares ISA	4700	4500		9200
Sub-Total	**8600**	**9500**	**400**	**18500**
Policy value's				
Endowment policy			6450	6450
Sub-Total			**6450**	**6450**
Pension Funds (fund values)				
Private Pension	17800			17800
Sub-Total	**17800**			**17800**
Property				
Own home			180000	180000
Sub-Total			**180000**	**180000**
Cars				
Marks car	6000			**6000**
Julies car		5500		**5500**
Sub -Total	**6000**	**5500**		**11500**
Other				
Furnishings			20000	**20000**
Jewellery	300	1200		**1500**
Sub-Total	**300**	**1200**	**20000**	**21500**
TOTAL ASSETS	**32700**	**16200**	**206850**	**255750**
Liabilities				
Mortgage			-90000	**-90000**
Car loan	-1200	-1000		**-2200**
Visa	-300			**-300**
Sub-Total	**-1500**	**-1000**	**-90000**	**-92500**
TOTAL LIABILITIES	**-1500**	**-1000**	**-90000**	**-92500**
NET WORTH	**31200**	**15200**	**116850**	**163250**

TABLE 2	Mark	Julie	Joint	TOTAL
Liquid Assets				
Bank Accounts	900	800	400	2100
Cash ISA's	3000	4200		7200
Stocks & Shares ISA	4700	4500		9200
Sub-Total	**8600**	**9500**	**400**	**18500**
Policy value's				
Endowment policy			6450	6450
Sub-Total			**6450**	**6450**
Pension Funds (fund values)				
Prudential Pension	17800			17800
Sub-Total	**17800**			**17800**
Property				
Own home			180000	180000
Sub-Total			**180000**	**180000**
Cars				
Marks car	6000			**6000**
Julies car		5500		**5500**
Sub -Total	**6000**	**5500**		**11500**
Other				
Furnishings			20000	**20000**
Jewellery	300	1200		**1500**
Sub-Total	**300**	**1200**	**20000**	**21500**
TOTAL ASSETS	**32700**	**16200**	**206850**	**255750**
Liabilities				
MORTGAGE			-90000	**-90000**
CAR LOAN	-1200	-1000		**-2200**
VISA	-300			**-300**
Sub-Total	**-1500**	**-1000**	**-90000**	**-92500**
TOTAL LIABILITIES	**-1500**	**-1000**	**-90000**	**-92500**
NET WORTH	**31200**	**15200**	**116850**	**163250**

Another name for this is 'passive income'. When you can build your passive income to be big enough to cover your expenditure then you technically don't have to work anymore. Passive income can be created by having sufficient assets in your bank account or investments to fund the rest of your years. It could be from rental income, investment returns or interest rates and/or pension income.

You could even develop passive income from selling books! Which reminds me, don't you think this book would make a good present for someone? Nudge nudge, hint hint!!

When you have a view of your net worth statement and put your expenditure sheet alongside it you can now see how close you are to the goal of achieving this. You can see your expenditure as X and you can see the assets producing Y.

Obviously, if you have very little in terms of assets then you will be a long way away from financial freedom. If your expenses are £2000 per month and the only asset is a bank account producing a few pence per month in interest then this ain't going to make you feel like it's time to start taking it easy.

Another way of looking at it is to consider each asset as an employee that works for you and helps you create an income that you don't have to physically work for. Effectively, these 'employees' are putting

"Financial freedom is having an income that covers your expenditure without having to do something you don't want to do in order to get it."

free fuel in your car for the journey. However, your debts are liabilities that make a hole in the fuel tank which therefore reduces the journey. The more employees (income generating assets) you have and the fewer holes (liabilities) you have the more your 'unearned' income will rise and so the further you can go.

This concept can also tie in to your attitude to investment risk (explained in chapter 8 – Turning on the Turbo) as it will help you to decide which assets produce the right level of returns to achieve this. For example, if you want to generate £30,000 per year in unearned income then you need £3 million in assets that return 1% or £300,000 in assets that return 10%. Obviously, 10% sounds better but you will probably have to take a higher level of investment risk to achieve 10%.

So, once you have created your own net worth table, have a good look at your assets that are producing income, interest or capital growth and then try to calculate the average return from these assets. This makes it easy to see if you need to redistribute your assets in any way to produce a better net return.

For example, I recently created a financial plan for a client who had accumulated a large property portfolio. His career meant he often had to move around and, rather than sell the properties he owned, he decided to rent them out and purchase a new property in his new location. Without going into too much detail (and not keeping the facts to the penny for confidentiality) the client owned 5 properties worth approx £1.1 million. The total mortgage debt on these 5 houses was just over £750,000. The rental income from these properties was around £35,000 but the monthly mortgage costs were around the same. So, in essence, the client was not really making any income from the £350,000 equity he had built up in his assets - which was a real waste.

We looked at different scenarios to attempt to reduce the liabilities whilst increasing the profit. We looked at lowering some of the mortgage interest rates. We also established that selling the properties that had low rent for the value of the property and using the equity to purchase properties that would produce a better return (for example a £200,000 house returning £750 per month rent was not as good as two £100,000 houses that produced £500 each). We also created an aggressive overpayment plan to reduce the debts as quickly as possible. Over a 5 year period, and by using a mixture of the above recommendations, we established that it was possible to create a rental income of £35000 per year above the costs – FROM THE SAME AMOUNT OF ASSETS (plus the overpayments of course).

Financial freedom (the amount the client needed to live in the way he desired) equated to £50,000 per year. These changes meant that he was now 70% there from this one asset class.

Finally, this conveniently leads on to the final benefit of producing a net worth statement.

Are you over or under exposed in any areas?

A net worth statement allows you to see how much exposure you have to each asset/liability class to determine whether you have too many eggs in one basket.

Due to the nature of home ownership being a desire in this country many people's net worth may look something like this –

Property £200,000   (or 80%)

Cash in bank £10,000   (or 4%)

Pension pot £30,000   (or 12%)

Investments £10,000   (or 4%)

This may seem ok but let me ask you this question..........What if property prices take a tumble? A 10% drop would create some damage don't you agree?

Also, look at the value of the pension fund. At a mere 12% this is unlikely to generate a big enough income to create financial freedom so the client will probably have to sell the property and downsize should this still be the case at 65

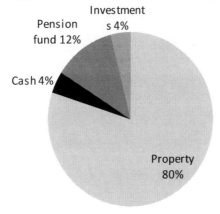

Typical Net Worth Pie Chart

I genuinely believe that equity release, or even downsizing of properties, will be used far more often as an option for retirement planning in the future as people place higher percentages of their total assets into property than they do into other assets such as pensions and investments. We will discuss retirement planning in more detail in chapter 9 but, for now, just consider how much of your total assets are tied up in your home. If, like many, it's the vast majority of your wealth then **be aware that it may not stay in your ownership too long into retirement!**

Monitoring your progress.

The final benefit of creating a net worth statement is that you can use it to monitor your progress by re-assessing your net worth on an annual basis. This helps you to ensure you are moving in the right direction. If you're net worth is growing it's a good indication that you are living within your means and building up assets that you can call upon for your goals and needs later in life. If it is declining (when you need it to grow) you can then analyse why it's declining and try and stop the leaks. Maybe you're spending more than you're earning? Maybe you're over exposed to asset classes that are volatile and need to diversify a little more? Maybe you need to re-schedule debt and try to reduce the interest rates you're paying?

Remember though that an ideal net worth chart does not just have to grow, it can also decline. Building wealth and accumulating assets may be the focus of your financial planning in your younger years but there is also a strong case for allowing your assets/net worth to decline during your later years. Remember when I talked about 'your bucket' in the last chapter and explained that the aim of a good financial plan is to enable you to do all the things you want to do in life without running out of money? I also mentioned that it's possible to die and leave money in the bucket that you didn't use for your life experiences because you were holding on to it.

Well in your later years (maybe post retirement) it's perfectly legitimate for you to plan a slow decline in assets so that you don't die with too much. For the average person (what I mean by average is someone that accumulates a net worth of between £100,000 and £1 million) this has the effect of not only maximising your life but also ensuring you don't die and leave an inheritance tax liability. If you are good with excel you could even create a chart that plots your growth like this.

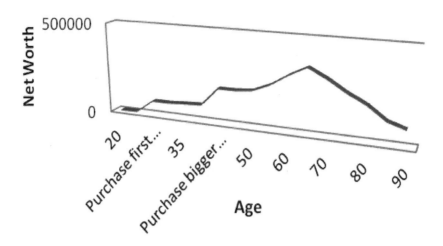

To monitor your progress as above then all you need to do is choose a date each year where you re-assess your net worth so you can chart the progress on an annual basis. Maybe this is something you could do if you have some quiet time between Christmas and New Year or even at the start of each new tax year?

So, to summarise, having a net worth statement allows you to see, in one foul swoop

- where you are on the journey
- which assets are working for you and which aren't
- if you are over exposed in any one asset class
- how close to financial freedom you are

and monitoring your net worth ensures

- you don't run out of money too fast

- you don't die and leave too much and miss out on things you could have achieved.

- whether you're going in the right direction or not

Now onto chapter 4...The Importance of having an emergency fund.

Chapter 4 – The Importance of an Emergency Fund

It is far better to foresee even without certainty than not to foresee at all.

~Henri Poincare

In chapter 1 we compared the financial planning process to that of planning a long car journey. Chapter 2 was organising your finances so that you can set off on the journey prepared and organised. Chapter 3 was compared to setting your milometer to zero when you leave the house. To continue the travel theme therefore chapter 4, the importance of an emergency fund, is the equivalent of checking your car before you set off.

Car experts suggest that before we embark on a long journey we should check the tyre thread, tyre pressure, oil levels, water levels, windscreen wipers and make sure the spare wheel is ok. Why do they suggest this? Well it's to make sure that your journey is not delayed by little problems.

In the financial planning process checking your car before you set off is the equivalent of having an emergency fund.

An emergency fund is an amount of money that you put to one side in order to cover life's little financial problems. Problems such as the

"Little problems insufficiently prepared for can become BIG problem."

central heating boiler bursting, your car needing a new engine, you lose your job or you have an accident or illness that stops you from earning etc. You see, little problems insufficiently prepared for can become BIG problems, potentially ruining the whole trip.

Would you put your family in the car and set off on your trip if you knew the car had no oil? Would you drive off knowing you had a puncture? Of course not. Why? Because it's cheaper to buy some oil than replace an engine... and a new tyre is cheaper than a new wheel and suspension unit right?

Here's another question. If your boiler bursts in the morning and your child comes home from school the same day with a letter saying the school ski trip (that you promised they could go on this year) will cost you £500 this week would you be able to cover the costs or would you be borrowing the cash to pay for them?

You may think this is an unfortunate week by normal standards but how many times has something like this happened? I bet you can remember times in your life when a few things have gone wrong all at once and its set you back financially. The question is how far will it take you off your course? Will it just delay you a short while or will it make you abandon your journey? A delay is acceptable, abandoning your journey isn't.

What will determine the effect of whether this becomes a delay or an abandonment will be whether you have an emergency fund or not, because it's your emergency fund that will stop you from having to go onto the red, borrow the money or tell your little one they can't go skiing with all their school friends.

So that's why having an emergency fund is the next step in the financial planning process. It helps you to complete your journey even if a tyre bursts!

So how do you develop an emergency fund?

If you don't have savings already then the obvious way to develop an emergency fund is to start with what was discussed in chapter 2 – Budgeting. Here the importance of establishing your disposable income was highlighted so you can start to use it towards your goals and/or needs. It's this spare cash that I would suggest that you *initially* start to save in order to provide your emergency fund (or safety net). Yes I know we talked about allocating funds towards your goals and value's but it's far more important to build up a safety net first. Do you think a trapeze artist tries his first somersault without a net? Of course not, there probably wouldn't be a show if they did!

According to the Aviva family finances report released in May 2012 only 37% of families are saving for a rainy day, and only 19% of families save on a monthly basis. So, if you can establish a budget and get organised with your disposable income, you will be in a minority of people who are building up assets for your future and getting ahead in the game.

In fact, in another survey from 2012, this time produced by the personal asset lender Borro, it shows that the average adult has just £1574 in savings and 27% of people have no savings at all. So you don't need to save for too long to be 'above average' do you?

How much should you keep in an emergency fund?

Most experts agree that you should keep between *3 and 6 months* of your living expenses set aside for an emergency fund. However, this can vary based on what insurance you have in place, whether or not you have children and what debt you have. I would also suggest that you find out what benefits are available from your employer as that can make a big difference, especially for long term illness issues.

If you are a single person with no children and good company sick pay then the need for an emergency fund can be restricted purely to having cash for last minute purchases or breakdown problems etc. Three months expenditure may be sufficient for you.

If you are self-employed with a family and no sick pay then your emergency fund needs to be higher to cover the above problems PLUS protection against periods of time off work etc. This is where you may want to work towards having six months expenditure rather than three.

If you've retired and your income has dropped after finishing work then you may need a higher emergency fund as it's not as easy to replenish it if you're not earning as much.

The reason you want to have three to six months of expenses saved up is that the most common reason for the need of an emergency fund is due to a sudden loss of income. If you or your spouse loses your job(s) you still have bills to pay and it may take a few months to find suitable new employment. Remember, by preparing for a worst case scenario the smaller emergencies such as replacing the hot water heater that just broke down will be easily covered.

Where should you put your emergency fund?

Because you may need access to this money at any time it's important that you don't use accounts that penalise you for taking the money out before a set time. Whilst it may be tempting to go for the higher rates that often come with 6 or 12 month notice accounts, it may work against you when you need the cash as there will often be a penalty.

Cash ISA's with instant access are good products to use for emergency funds as the rates can be competitive and any growth will be tax free. Unfortunately, cash ISA's do have a limit on what you can contribute each year (the 2013/2014 Cash ISA limit is £5760 with the overall annual ISA limit being £11520) but this should be fine unless you have a need for a very high fund.

Don't forget you can have a cash ISA each if you're a couple and, if you're fortunate to use up your full allowance each year, you can soon build up a nice little tax free fund.

If you've identified you have a need for a large emergency fund then you could set aside two separate pots for this purpose. One could provide you with immediate access and one could have limited access (an emergency

emergency fund if you like!). This could help you get better rates/returns on your second pot or you could even invest into funds with higher potential returns like stocks and shares ISAs. I suppose that's like carrying an emergency parachute if the first one doesn't fix the problem.

If you currently don't have an emergency fund or find it difficult to save money the key is to start small. You have to realize that accumulating one month's worth of expenses may take some time, let alone three to six months, but if you set your immediate goals to be small and manageable you will have a better chance in reaching them.

The final tip I'd like to give on the subject of an emergency fund is to make sure you replenish the fund when it's accessed. It's OK when something goes wrong and the emergency fund rescues you out of a bad situation, but it's highly likely that won't be the only problem you ever have. So continue to save. Like an emergency wheel that you only use until your puncture is fixed, your emergency fund is not something you should be dipping into for normal expenditure. That's what your current account is for so use that instead.

Finally, let me tell you a true story about a guy called Scooby so you can see why having an emergency fund is important.

Scooby is a young man who went to take money out of his bank. He only wanted £10 so he put his card in the cash machine and took it out. Scooby, unfortunately, is not very good at managing his money as he didn't realise he only had £9 left in his bank account. A short while later he received a letter from his bank stating that he owed them £28 in charges for an unarranged borrowing fee. He ignored it and put it in his drawer. A short while later he received another letter. He ignored it and put it in the drawer gain. This happened for a couple of years until Scooby's £1 overdrawn account eventually cost him around £600, and all because he didn't have an emergency fund.

Do you want to know what the long term effects of having no emergency fund is? DEBT!

The long term effect of having no emergency fund is DEBT!

Let's face it, if you have to buy something and you don't have the cash it's easy these days just to borrow it isn't it? Just put it on the credit card or get a loan.

You could even go into one of those ever increasing number of shops that are opening who provide 'pay day' or 'fast loans'. You know the ones, you borrow £200 and they take your family hostage at gunpoint unless you give them £300 back at the end of the month! OK, I exaggerate a little but you know what I mean. The 3000% APR schemes that are popping up in the town centres and on TV, usually between programs like Jeremy Kyle and Loose Women! These days all you need to do is make a phone call or stick your card in a wall and you can have someone else's money within seconds.

So what are the long term effects of debt? Simple, less disposable income! If you have other people taking their money back as soon as you get yours that leaves you with less to use towards YOUR goals and they get more towards theirs.

What's the long term effect of less disposable income? Less chance of living the life you want today AND tomorrow.

To end this chapter I just want to give you two stories side by side to really get this message across.

Let's meet two brothers, Johnny and Joe. Both are on a journey of different sorts.

1. Johnny decides he wants to take his family to Scotland for the weekend. Joe decides he wants to save for his daughter's wedding.

2. Johnny sets off after putting the hotel postcode into his satellite navigation system and then filling up his petrol tank. Joe decides to put £50 per month away into a savings plan for a 15 year term as he thinks that will cover the costs of the wedding.

3. Johnny gets an oil warning light after 50 miles in the car. Joe gets an unexpected bill from the tax man.

4. Johnny ignores the oil light, thinking he will have a look at it when he needs to fill up again. Joe put's the letter from Her Majesty's revenue and customs behind the clock on the mantelpiece.

5. Johnny starts to smell burning but can't think what it is. Joe gets another letter and thinks 'oh yeah I need to sort it'.

6. Johnny finally runs out of fuel and stops at a petrol station. When he gets out he smells the burning even more so he checks under the bonnet to see his engine is steaming. Luckily there's a mechanic in the garage who has a look at it and he tells him his engine has burnt out by

driving it with no oil. Final result, a new engine and a spoilt holiday. Joe gets a third letter and finally decides to read it fully. His bill states he owes £800 for a miscalculation on his tax return and this has now risen by £200 for late payment fees. Final result, he cashes in the £50 savings to cover his bill and the daughter's now getting married at a registry office.

Can you see what I'm getting at? Not having an emergency fund can stop you from reaching your goals and little problems that are unprepared for (and handled badly) can become bigger problems.

So, start looking at your budget again and revisit where the leaks are in your bucket. It's an important foundation for any long term plan. After all, how safe would you feel if you kept driving with no oil, no thread on your tyres and no spare wheel?

So to summarise -

1. Develop an emergency fund of 3-6 months expenditure.

2. Keep an emergency fund in an account that can get you the best rate of interest with immediate access.

3. If you feel you need a large emergency fund then there's nothing wrong with having 2.

   One with immediate access for when money is required (that's not available from your current account) and one that can be used after that (when higher amounts are required). The second one can then be invested or placed in accounts with higher returns in return for more limited access.

4. If you have to draw on your emergency fund for whatever reason fill it back up to the previous level as soon as possible.

Now onto chapter 5 - Ditch the Debt.

Chapter 5 – Ditch the Debt

"Some debts are fun when you are acquiring them,

but none are fun when you set about retiring them."

~Ogden Nash

Remember the good old days? You know the ones. The days where you could watch daytime TV without someone telling you that your life will be so much better if you just give in to your urges and borrow their money at an extortionate interest rate? You know, the days when people said

"*Borrowing money does not create freedom, it creates bondage"*

'if you haven't got the money then you can't afford it'? Well how times have changed.

Debt, today, is a major part of society. I can't believe that trading standards are now allowing VISA adverts to suggest that borrowing money gives us 'freedom'. That's like allowing McDonalds to suggest that, if you eat in their restaurants every day, you'll lose weight!

Borrowing money does not create freedom, it creates bondage! The book of proverbs written almost 3000 years ago by King Solomon, reputedly the wisest man that had ever lived, stated that a borrower is a servant to the lender. Guess what? Nothing's changed since!

We only need to look at the recent credit crunch to see the effect that debt can have if not properly controlled.

In 2010-11 government receipts were around £548 billion yet the expenditure was £697 billion, of which £44 billion is debt interest. That works out at over £5 million an hour! YES, £5 MILLION AN HOUR JUST FOR THE INTEREST (I shouted that!).

In 2012 we have made some slight improvements. Income was around £592 billion and expenditure was at £683 billion – so we only had to borrow £91 billion this year! Can you imagine if your household lived this way?

So, in 2010 your family income was £54,800 and your expenditure was £69,700 and, in 2012, your family income was £59,200 and your expenditure was £68,300. Doesn't take long to get in a financial mess by living that way does it? The only difference with us and the government fiscal policy is that you and I can't raise taxes when we need people to pay us more!

In a recent TV documentary on channel 4 entitled 'Britain's Trillion Pound Horror Story,' the reporter Martin Durkin revealed the full extent of the financial mess we are in. Want to have a guess at how much the UK owes as a country?

It's an estimated £4.8 trillion!

In figures that's £4,800,000,000,000,000. To put that into context, if everyone in the UK sold their homes it still wouldn't be enough to pay off the debt. Hmm.....maybe I should've sent them the chapter on having an emergency fund?

This chapter is therefore all about removing or reducing your debt and the reasons why. You see chapter 1 (creating your lifeline) was the equivalent of planning your journey and chapter 2 (budgeting) was putting the fuel in the tank. Chapter 3 (emergency fund) was checking the car before you set off and chapter 5 was about understanding your staring point. Chapter 5 - Ditch the Debt, is therefore the equivalent of releasing the hand break!

Have you ever started to drive away in your car and felt something was holding you back? Like you're driving through deep mud or up a really steep hill? Only to find out you've left the hand break on. Obviously, as a man this has never happened to me but I have heard of others doing it (ahem).

Well that scenario is the equivalent of trying to build up your financial assets whilst in debt.

Trying to go somewhere when something is holding you back will mean that, not only will you use more petrol, but you will also get there more slowly.

To move forward in life – ditch the debt

That's why 'ditch the debt' is the next step in your financial planning process. The reason that it is applied early on in the 10 steps is because there is no point putting more money into bank accounts or savings that earn a small amount of interest if you are paying 3-4 times that amount in debt interest on your existing loans.

Now I'm not saying allocate everything to debt but it is usually a very good idea to allocate a decent amount. It's especially important to allocate funds to short term debts as, if you can pay them off quickly,

> *There is no point putting more money into bank accounts or savings that earn a small amount of interest if you are paying 3-4 times that amount in debt interest on your loans.*

you can then release the monthly payments they were taking to be used for other purposes.

As of writing this, a half decent bank account or cash ISA will pay around 2-3% in interest (don't forget to take tax off this rate if you are a taxpayer and/or not in an ISA). A decent loan rate is around the 6-8% mark. Assuming you have the emergency fund sorted then simply growing it further instead of paying down your debt will lose you 4-5% per year. So instead, pay off the debt and do something with the extra money it releases.

For example, let's presume you have a loan with £3000 outstanding and the monthly repayments are £250 for another 12 months. By analysing your budget you have identified a further £250 that can also be allocated to this debt. By paying a total of £500 per month to the loan then it's reasonable to assume you'll now repay the debt in half the time. Not only will this save you the interest that you would've paid in the final 6 months but you will also have £500 spare that you can then allocate to your goals from month 7.

Result!

Please note this is a simplistic calculation as a loan of £3000 with 12 repayments of £250 is effectively interest free, giving no real savings of interest in the above example. In reality there needs to be a calculation done by asking your lender for total costs of interest if you choose to follow this option. You can then calculate what savings of interest will be made.

One area that this can be extremely beneficial is with a mortgage. As I write this the Bank of England's interest rate is 0.5% (why am I now imagining someone reading this in 10 years and saying "only 0.5% - wow?"). A few years ago the rate was 5.75%.

An interest only mortgage of £100,000 at today's rate of 0.5% costs a mere £41.66 per month. Three years ago that would've been £479.16 – a difference of £437.50 per month.

Want to guess what most people do with savings like this when their debt repayments drop?

Nothing......it just disappears into their normal everyday expenditure. But what if that £437 would've been paid into the mortgage as an overpayment? Well let's see in the following graph–

Loan Graph Illustration

Loan Amount £100000

Events Applied Overpay mortgage by £437 per month from Year 1 to year 25

Result Loan paid off in less than 9 years

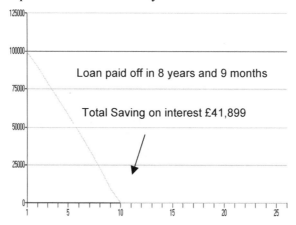

That's right. By using the monthly saving from the reduction in interest rates the mortgage would be totally repaid in under 9 years and, instead of paying almost £42000 to the bank, that can now be put into your pocket and redirected to your goals.

Believe me, I have seen this situation a lot and, in some cases, have managed to help some clients be hundreds of thousands of pounds better off by redirecting debt repayments and reversing the compound interest rates. Hundreds of thousands you ask? Well they must have really big mortgages then? Not really because we haven't looked at the second step in reversing the compound interest process.

Look at the previous graph again. It shows that a 25 year mortgage will be paid off in 8 years 9 months with a monthly overpayment of £437. So what will happen if this amount of £437 is now redirected into savings with a net return of 5% per annum for the next 16 years (that they would have paid to the mortgage if interest rates rose again).

£437 per month invested over 16 years with a 5% net return would give you £127,394.80. Let me repeat that - £127,394.80. Not bad eh? Maybe that would help with one or two of the goals on your lifeline?

So, now you can see the long term effects of ditching the debt let's look at 6 basic rules when it comes to borrowing money…if you have to.

Rule no.1 – ask yourself 'do you really NEED it'?

In other words are you borrowing money for something that you need or just something you want?

If it's a 'want' then total up the total amount of money you're going to pay for the item **with all the interest added on** and then decide if you still want it!

For example, I recently saw a 47 inch flat screen TV in a store window. The shop will be nameless but, basically, it's one of these that sell reconditioned goods and allow you to pay for them weekly so they sound really affordable. The cash price was £1276.44 but, if you wanted, you could put 10% down and just pay just £12.67 per week for 140 weeks. That sounds a lot easier that doesn't it? I mean £12.67 a week? – Surely that's a lot better than taking £1267 out of your account right? Well, once again, let's have a look at the facts:

£12.67 X 140 weeks = £ 1773.80. So that's another £500 on top of the original price.

But what if it breaks down I hear you ask? Ah, well no need to worry. For a meagre £6.82 per week you get 'service cover'. This now takes the total cost to £2728.60 for a 47 inch flat screen TV. What makes me laugh here is that the £6.82 service cover over 140 weeks is another £954.80 so you're almost paying the same amount for the service cover as you are for the telly. You could've bought a new one with it!!

Let's now take this a stage further and use the example when buying a car, using the following stats

1. Purchase price of car £10000 (no inflation/RPI included so the car is always £10000 to keep things simple)

2. Deposit of £2000 based on the part exchange of the car bought 4 years ago for £10000 (it's called depreciation I'm afraid!!)

3. Repeat the purchase every 4 years.

Option 1 is pay cash for the car by saving up £8000 in, for example, a cash ISA over 4 years and receive 3% tax free growth per annum. The amount you would need to save therefore would be £157 per month.

Option 2 is borrow the money but pay 9% interest on the loan so the cost will therefore be £199 per month.

This is a difference of £42 per month. Now this still may seem an acceptable difference and something that won't affect your lifestyle too badly. But what if we then multiply this £42 per month over a 50 year driving career? The difference between these two 'choices' is now **£25,200**. And what if you are a 2 car family? What else could you have done with that **£50,000**? What if you add this £50000 to the £140000 saved on the mortgage? See what I mean now?

The different effect compounds over time to make a big difference don't they? In fact someone once described compound interest as the 'eighth wonder of the world'.

Rule no. 2 - if you are going to borrow then SHOP AROUND

Don't accept the first option given to you. There are many internet comparison sites these days which can provide quick and easy methods to find the lowest borrowing rates. A 5 minute search could save hundreds of pounds. In fact I've just done a quick comparison on a £1000 loan over 5 years and, on one page, the interest rates varies from 7.6% APR to 53.9% APR. This resulted in a difference of over £200 per month for the 5 year term (or around £12000 in total). How many hours will it take you to earn that amount after tax? Worth your time shopping around do you think?

Also, whilst it's ok to have a good relationship with your bank, don't feel that's the first place you should go to if you need a loan. Sure, get a quote from them but then compare to what's available elsewhere. Banks rely on laziness like this to make money and sometimes play the 'loyalty' card when selling their wares. However, they can't always have the best rate all the time can they?

The other thing to be aware of here is your ability to be strong under pressure. In

"Borrowing on an appreciating asset is called investing and increases your wealth. Borrowing on a depreciating asset is called spending and decreases your wealth".

my experience I have found that the higher the interest rate you are offered the more convincing the salesperson. Never make a decision like this on an emotion or in a rush or because someone is trying to convince you it's a good idea to make a decision there and then. Make the decision based on the numbers, the lower the better and, if you have to walk away from the deal walk away.

Even better is to negotiate and put the ball back in their corner. If you can find a better rate elsewhere show them and ask them to beat it. Honestly, you'll be surprised what you can save when you try.

Rule no. 3 – know the true cost of borrowing

The example above shows you the importance of working out the total cost before rushing in.

Check out the APR (annual percentage rate) as this is the true cost of borrowing the money.

The APR includes important factors such as:

- the interest rate you must pay;

- how you repay the loan; the length of the loan agreement (or term); frequency and timing of instalment payments; and amount of each payment; and

- certain fees associated with the loan.

All lenders have to tell you what their APR is before you sign an agreement. The APR will vary from lender to lender; generally, the lower the APR the better the deal for you.

Rule no. 4 – to make borrowing work for you try to restrict borrowing to assets that will appreciate.

Borrowing on an appreciating asset is called investing and increases your wealth. Borrowing on a depreciating asset is called spending and decreases your wealth.

Mortgages are the most common form of borrowing on appreciating assets as, over time, property generally rises in value. This is fine and acceptable. Of course if you can pay cash for a property even better but it's not exactly the norm in the early years of a person's adult life. The problem comes when you borrow on depreciating assets as in the car example already given.

I have many friends and clients who have significantly improved their net worth as well as their income by investing in properties and borrowing the money on buy to let mortgages to achieve it. Not only are they having the mortgage paid by their rent but they are also able to enjoy the capital appreciation when property prices rise. I am not going to go into detail about how to do it in this book (maybe another one) but, in general, borrowing money on an appreciating asset can be a good thing. However you do need to know what you're doing; don't just do it because your friend did. Remember, risk comes from not knowing what you're doing ok?

It is also occasionally in your favour to borrow if the interest rate you will pay is lower than the interest you are receiving on your cash (this is rare but can happen) and there are also occasions when it can be in your interest to invest spare cash as opposed to paying it all off debt.

I recently spoke to some clients of mine in the office who had some money to invest. Their intention was 'to make the most of it' so we looked at their

"Risk comes from not knowing what you're doing".

circumstances. We established that they already had an emergency fund and they also had some savings in a 12 month bond so there was no need for immediate access.

We looked at their mortgage and found that the interest rate was 0.8% and, after completing our psychometric risk questionnaires, it revealed that they were both fairly speculative with their investment views. As a result of this we started to discuss investing the money for the medium to long term on the basis that the clients would be better off if their investments could increase by a net return of more than 0.8% per year.

There were other reasons for recommending this course of action too, such as the fact that they needed to develop some assets for their retirement but, in essence, the chance of a higher return than 0.8% was what triggered this course of action.

Should their debt have had an interest level of 8-9% then, even a speculative investor would have to really believe in their investment choices to guarantee an annual return better than this. If this is the case then you might be better off by clearing the debt and then allocating the monthly savings that you have from the debt repayments.

Rule no. 5 – pay off debts as quickly as possible.

The quicker you repay the debt the less interest you will pay in total (assuming there are no early encashment penalties). For more information on this then simply refer to the graph

If you have a debt problem then don't bury your head in the sand thinking it will go away. IT WON'T!

used at the beginning of this chapter where you can see the effects of paying a mortgage off early.

Rule no.6 – try to avoid adding short term debts like a car loan or overdraft onto longer term commitments like a mortgage.

This is another area where I see people making financial mistakes, the thought that having one low payment for an extended period is better than a higher payment for a short period. You know the adverts – 'consolidate your debts into one easy payment', 'simplify your finances by replacing many debts with one' blah, blah, blah!

Now I'm not saying that all the companies that advertise this way are bad nor am I saying that you won't be better off by using them. What I am saying is, if the monthly repayments are able to be paid, then simply calculate the total amount payable under your current plans and then calculate the total amount payable under the new scheme. Again, assuming you are able to afford the current payments, then stay where you are if the total cost is cheaper and only move if they are not.

It's the same with adding loans on to your mortgage. The interest rate on a mortgage may be lower but it will still cost you more if you extend the term of the debt over a long period. What would you rather pay - £200 per month over 3 years or £50 per month over 20? You know what? I'm not going to give you the answer. Just get a calculator out and do the maths.

You should only choose this option if you are struggling to meet your payments or you are able to transfer the monthly loan repayments onto the mortgage so you don't extend the term and benefit from a lower rate on all the debt and therefore reduce the term. An example of this is transferring a loan of £200 per month with 3 years left that has an interest rate of 8% to your mortgage which is only costing you 4% BUT CONTINUING TO PAY the

£200 so that it can be cleared off in 2 years 6 months. This is a good option if the numbers work in your favour but, again, make sure you crunch the numbers first.

Rule no.7 - never try to borrow your way out of debt

Certain institutions are recommending this as a way of 'getting out of debt'. That's like trying to dig yourself out of a hole if you're not careful! Instead, contact someone like the Citizens Advice Bureau who can provide free advice on how to resolve the issue in the most suitable and unbiased way.

If you do have a debt problem then don't bury your head in the sand thinking it will go away. IT WON'T! Go get some advice and start a debt reduction process. Just make sure they give you a ladder to get out the hole rather than a spade.

Never try to dig yourself out of debt!

How to get out of debt.

A debt reduction process can take different forms. Here are a couple of examples:-

Case Study

Mr 'Borrower' has a car loan and 2 visa cards. He owes £500 on one visa card, £1050 on the other and £9000 on the car loan. He pays £50 per month to each visa, which pays the interest only (doesn't reduce the debt) and he pays £200 per month on his car loan which has 4 years remaining.

After creating his budget he realises he has £200 spare each month that he can allocate to a debt reduction programme (he already has an emergency fund). To reduce the debt as quickly as possible he could do the following-

Method 1 – Start with the small debts first

1. Mr Borrower could pay the full £200 per month to visa 1 meaning that the £200 on top of the £50 will clear off the debt in 2 months.

2. In month 3 Mr Borrower can now allocate £350 to the second visa card (£50 existing, £200 new payment + £50 spare that was going to visa card no.1). This will then clear off visa no.2 in another 3 months (3x350=1050).

3. In month no. 6 Mr Borrower now has £350 per month to allocate as an overpayment to the car loan, giving a total payment of £550. Allocating this to the car loan will clear the debt in 15 months, saving

over £1100 in interest payments at a rate of 9%. That's not all. Guess what else it does? It also gives him £550 per month from month 21 to save so he can purchase his next car cash!

Method 2 – Start with the highest interest rates first

Another option Mr Borrower could look at would be to repay the debt with the highest interest rate first. This, potentially, could save the highest level of interest but it needs to be compared with the option above (where he starts with the lowest debt first) to see which would either save most money and/or pay off all the debts in the shortest time period.

Let's say you have two credit cards.

1. Credit Card A has a £3,000 balance and a 22% interest rate.
2. Credit Card B has a £1,500 balance and a 12% interest rate.

Let's also assume you can spend £150 a month toward these debts. If you pay off Credit Card A first, you'd pay a total of £1,283 in interest and it would take 39 months to become debt free. On the other hand, if you paid off Credit Card B first, you'd pay a total of £1,764 in interest and it would take you 42 months to become debt free.

Paying off the high interest rate debt therefore saves you £481 in interest and you'll pay off the debt 3 months sooner.

To determine which option is best is difficult without knowing all the circumstances of the debts i.e. amounts, interest rates etc.

In general I would say that the first option is great for seeing quicker results, releasing more disposable income and helping you to stay motivated (as you see the small debts paid off quicker).

The second option is possible the best overall option if you want to achieve the maximum savings in overall interest payments.

So, there's a brief synopsis on 'ditching the debt'. Remember, if you want to move forward it's hard to do it when things are holding you back. So release the hand break!

To summarise –

1. Understand that debt is bondage and that it can hold you back from reaching your goals.

2. Only borrow after you've asked yourself if you REALLY need it.

3. If you are going to borrow then shop around for the best deal.

4. Know the true cost of borrowing (APR) and choose a loan based on the numbers – the lower the better.

5. Try and restrict borrowing to assets that appreciate and avoid borrowing on assets that depreciate.

6. Pay off debts as quickly as possible to reduce the interest.

7. Avoid adding short term debts on to longer term commitments

8. Don't try and borrow your way out of debt – seek professional help if you are struggling to keep up repayments.

Now onto chapter 6 – Build a House of Stone.

Chapter 6 – Building a House of Stone

"I detest life-insurance agents; they always argue that I shall someday die, which is not so."

~Stephen Leacock

OK, so we've planned our journey, organised our budget, established what we're worth, built an emergency fund and started to get out of debt. If you're anything like me you'll probably think it's now time to drive off and start moving towards the landmarks on your journey right? (yes I'm afraid I was one of those kids that did used to sit in the back seat asking 'how many more miles?' every 10 minutes). Well hang on, there's one more question that needs to be asked before you hit the road.....

....ARE YOU INSURED?

In the UK it's illegal to drive without insurance. The reason this rule is enforced is not just for your benefit (i.e. someone steals your car etc) but also for the benefit of others who may be affected by your mistakes or mishaps. You are not legally required to have contents insurance but you must have buildings insurance if you have a mortagage, so why the difference? Well, as I've just said, it's about protecting others from your unfortunate circumstances. If you live in a semi-detached house and you burn your settee then that's your problem. If you burn your house down, it's now also your lenders (and your neighbour's) problem!

So chapter 6 is all about insurance and protection or, as I call it....building your house of stone. The reason I refer to it as 'building a house of stone' is that it

> *Protection is more about protecting others that could suffer around you as it is about protecting you from your suffering.*

reminds me of the story of the 3 little pigs. Do you remember the 3 little pigs? One built a house of straw, one used wood and one used brick remember? Whose house was standing when the big bad wolf came and huffed and puffed? Well I'll give you a clue - it wasn't the one that was built of straw!

Building financial wealth can be related to building a house (we'll just park the car analogies for a minute). There's no point designing (creating your lifeline) and then costing (budgeting stage) for a beautiful home that will have no foundation (emergency fund) only for it all to fall down when a wolf comes, and believe me, wolves come to many people's lives.

But what are these wolves in financial terms?

Simple, they are anything that could sabotage the chances of you not being able to achieve the goals on your lifeline. The main four being death, disability, illness and redundancy.

Insurance also covers material items such as your house, your car and your valuables however, as this book is more about financial planning than insurance products, I will focus this chapter on how to protect against the four 'wolves' mentioned above.

First of all, understand that buying insurance is effectively a gamble. You weigh up the cost of the premiums against the risk of losing what is valuable and then decide which the least painful option is. With life assurance, and especially critical illness premiums, you could pay a lot

> *"Financial 'wolves' are any catastrophes that can sabotage the chances of you achieving your goals."*

of money and will hopefully not see any benefit apart from the peace of mind of knowing your loved ones and yourself are protected.

So whilst I am a big fan of being adequately protected, I personally would not want to be paying for more than I need. I believe that the focus, when assessing the need for protection, is to make sure that you and your loved ones are not affected financially whilst they're affected emotionally – be it a temporary loss or a permanent one. Ideally the outcome should be that the financial effects are minimised so you can continue on your journey. So, let's look at some of these wolves that we need to protect against.

Wolf No. 1 - Death

I'm sorry that we have to be a little morbid here but death is an unfortunate fact of life. According to the office of national statistics there were 493,242 deaths in England and Wales in 2010. That's over 1300 people every day.

32% of these were due to circulatory problems such as heart disease and strokes. In the UK thousands are killed or injured every week in road traffic accidents. I can think of 3 people who were in my school year who didn't make it past their mid-thirties.

The death of a parent will have a devastating effect on the family, and that's without even thinking about the financial issues. However, the good news is that the costs for pure life assurance are relatively low compared to the benefits it will provide (what I mean by pure life assurance is where the policy has no investment element attached to it, so endowment policies and whole of life plans will probably not fit into this category).

A healthy 30 year old couple can buy £100,000 of decreasing life assurance for 20 years for around £6.80 per month*. That's the equivalent of 22 pence per day. A level amount of £100,000 will cost £8.63* (I will explain the differences later in this chapter).

The need for life assurance

As previously mentioned, the main objective of life cover is to enable the dependents to maintain their lifestyle should a death occur. Essentially, dependents are people whose lifestyle is dependent on your earning capacity. The obvious people who come to mind here are spouses, partners and children. However, if you are a business owner you also need to think about the death of a business partner or maybe even a key person in the company. Have a think now about who would be affected financially if you were to die and also have a think about how you would be affected if certain people around you were to die. I know it's not a pleasant thought but these situations need to be considered.

As already mentioned, life assurance is a gamble where you pay the insurance company a premium each month and they offer to cover you if you die. So with this in mind let's use the 30 year old couple above to work out the risk vs reward calculation.

It will cost £8.63 per month to take out a policy that will cover both parties for an amount of £100,000. The gamble is therefore whether to pay £8.63 for 20 years (which is £2071.20) in return for a potential £100,000 pay out.

Depending on your circumstances you then have to decide if this is a 'good bet'. For example, if the 30 year old couple take the insurance out for a

"Build a strong house -
make sure your greatest assets are protected"

£100,000 mortgage yet they both earn £50,000 per year each then there is an argument that the dependent could survive without the partner's income. Granted, the lifestyle will reduce but not to a point of being poverty stricken.

However, let's now assume that the 30 year old couple both earn £25000 per annum and they have two small children. The effect of losing the partner in this situation will be devastating. It's highly likely that the survivor will struggle to maintain the mortgage payments and raise a family should this event happen.

The key, therefore, is assessing the risk and calculating how much you would need to maintain a decent standard of living should a loss occur, without spending a fortune and being over insured. Let's look at how we can calculate this.

*source The Exchange 22/06/2011

How much cover do you need?

I've never met a client who wants to be better off if their partner dies, they just don't want to be worse off. So, working on that principle, here's a little process you can go through to help you work out the amount of life insurance you will need –

1) Firstly, work out the debts you have which will need to be repaid?

ITEM	AMOUNT OF DEBT (£)
Mortgage	
Loans	
Funeral Expenses	
TOTAL	

This now gives you an initial amount of cover you will need in the form of a lump sum.

2) Now work out how much you will need to live on after the death of a partner by working out your living costs but deducting the survivors net income.

ITEM	MONTHLY COST (£)
Monthly living costs (use expenditure sheet from chapter 2)	
Minus Survivors income	
TOTAL ANNUAL SHORTFALL	

This now gives you the annual shortfall (if any) that you could provide for in the form of an income or, if you times the annual figure by the amount of years you need the cover for, it can be provided by increasing the lump sum.

Example, your joint annual expenditure is £30,000 per year but your partner earns £20,000 after tax, leaving a shortfall of £10,000 per year.

3) Work out how long you need the cover for.

The term of years you need the cover for will be determined by the amount of years you have the financial responsibilities. For example, the lump sums will probably be in line with the remaining terms of your debt and the income shortfall may be required until children become financially self- dependent.

4) Take away any existing cover

What I suggest you do now is add in any current life assurance provisions that you already have. This may be in the form of existing plans, employer death in service benefits (can be up to 4 times salary), pension funds and endowment policies, money in savings and any assets that can be sold. Take these figures away from the lump sum or income shortfalls and then you will have an accurate figure of the amount of cover you need.

Here's a full example:-

Kate and Darren are married with 2 children aged 7 and 5. Darren works as an engineer with a salary of £30,000 pa whist Kate is currently working part time in a local store for a wage of £7000 pa. They have a mortgage debt of £95,000 with 18 years remaining and two loans totalling £8,000 with 2 years remaining.

They have £3000 in savings. They have not made a will.

Assuming funeral costs of £5000 they will need a total of £108,000 of cover for the mortgage, loans and funeral.

However, Darren has a company pension scheme which will pay 2 times salary (£60,000) and the pension fund is valued at £18000 – which Kate should receive as he has nominated her on the beneficiary form with his employers.

The lump sum shortfall is therefore £30,000 (they don't want to use savings as they would want to keep that for future emergencies).

Lump Sum Death Benefit Requirement Calculation

Liability on£ Death	TOTALS	Cover required £	
Mortgage	95000		
Loans	8000		
Funeral Costs	5000	**108000 (A)**	

Assets on Death	£	TOTALS	
Savings	3000 (to be ignored)		
Pension fund	18000		
Death in Service	60000	**78000 (B)**	**30000 (A-B)**

Darren & Kate have also worked out that they need £1200 per month to maintain their lifestyle (assuming the loans and mortgage were paid off) and they will need this amount until their youngest child is 21.

This £1200 can either be used to replace part of Darren's income if he died (for Kate and the kids) or, if Kate dies, then it can be used to help Darren either take a different job that allows him to look after the children or it can be used to pay someone to work as a nanny so he can pursue his career. In essence, it will allow them to continue to maintain some form of lifestyle after their partner's death.

As their youngest is 5 they want this cover for 16 years. So the cover on Darren's life will need to be £14,400 times 16 years, a total of £230,400. However, Kate can continue to work in her part time job and still look after the children so her income shortfall is –

£14400 – 7000 = 7400 x 16 years = £118400.

Monthly income requirement calculation

		Per month	**Per year**
	Current monthly living costs	2000	24000
Minus	Reduction in living costs on death (due to debts being repaid and outgoings lower)	(800)	(9600)
	= Living costs for survivor	1200	14400
Minus	Income (583)		(7000)
	Annual Income Shortfall		**7400**
Times	No of years until children self dependent		x16
	Total lump sum shortfall		**118400**

The lump sum can be protected by a policy called 'decreasing term assurance' with a term of 16 years for a sum assured of £118,400 Alternatively, the income can be protected by something called a 'family income benefit policy' for an amount of £7400 per annum over 16 years – as this will pay the benefit as a monthly tax free income.

At current rates £7400 per annum of family income benefit for 16 years will cost around £6.45* for a 30 year old non- smoking couple. A lump sum of £118,400 on the same terms will cost £7.75.*

So, as you can see, basic life assurance (or term assurance with no investment return) is not expensive. The decision is whether you want to take the gamble of paying the premiums for the term of the policies and (hopefully) not get anything back or let the insurance company take the gamble of having to pay out the insured amount should you die.

*source exweb.exhange.uk.com 17/11/2010

One other thing to be aware of here is that any couples who aren't married may not be automatically entitled to death in service benefits should their partner die. Nor are they guaranteed guardianship of their children! If this is the case then make sure you make a will so that the trustees can interpret your wishes. Also, unmarried partners with assets above the inheritance threshold of £325,000 (in 2013-14) could also face an inheritance tax bill on their partner's estate.

So, that's wolf 1 kept at bay. Now we'll move onto wolf no. 2.

Wolf No.2 - Disability

Disability could arise out of a serious illness such as cancer, heart attack or stroke. It could also arise out of an accident. The effect of these wolves is that they could potentially stop you from earning a salary or generating business profits. If this is the case then you could consider taking out some insurance to cover this.

However, before we look at how to calculate the level of cover you need let's look at the chances of suffering from a disability or critical illness.

- Government statistics show that as of February 2009, there were over 2 million incapacity claimants who were unable to work due to illness or injury.

- Each year almost 220,000 people are diagnosed as new cancer registrations, which would qualify as a claim under the ABI standard illness definitions.*

- Up to age 65, a man has a 1 in 5 chance and a woman has a 1 in 6 chance of suffering a critical illness.*

- We are 5 times more likely to suffer from a serious illness than die before reaching age 65**

Sources: *ERC Frankona 2000/**Swiss RE 2000

When you look at the facts here it does get a little scary. I recently heard a statistic that everyone has been affected by cancer in some form or another. If it's not yourself then it will be someone close to you. I've personally lost both parents to cancer so I can believe this statement quite easily.

So how do we protect against this wolf? Well there are essentially two types of policy that can cover this. One is called critical illness cover and one is called permanent health insurance.

Critical Illness cover

Critical illness plans can cover both an income need as well as a lump sum need whilst permanent health insurance (also known as income protection policies) essentially provides for a replacement income only. Both these plans can be more expensive than life assurance due to the claims history mentioned above but critical illness can be added to a life assurance policy so you have both benefits in one plan –and this is often much cheaper to have both benefits on one plan rather than having separate policies.

A critical illness plan will generally pay out on the diagnosis of a critical illness specified in the policy document and following a survival period of 14-28 days. Even if you make a full recovery you can keep the money paid to you. However, I would urge you to compare the definitions of cover on critical illness plans. As of writing this we are awaiting the results of an extremely unfortunate accident for one of our clients where they may have to lose a limb. If this happens then it will trigger a critical illness claim for the client but we have noticed of late that one or two providers are now stating that it needs to be 'loss of 2 limbs' before a claim becomes eligible. A big difference isn't it for what you would think is essentially the same policy?!

When applying for any form of insurance it's also vital that you disclose all relevant matters on the application form. For example, in response to the insurance company's questions, if the applicant fails to disclose that his father died of a heart attack aged 55 or that he is having medical tests then the insurance company will wrongly assess the risks it is being asked to insure.

There have been repeated newspaper articles about people who claim on their critical illness policy only to have it turned down on an apparent technicality – the inference being that the insurance company cannot be trusted.

The truth is that behind every story of rejection there's a harrowing story of illness, distress and sorrow - and a potential story for the journalist. But that in itself is not evidence that the insurance company is guilty of devious behaviour. Yes insurance companies do make mistakes, but more often than not the claim was invalid from the outset.

Policyholder's have also been upset when claiming on critical illness policies to find that their illness is not one of the critical illnesses scheduled in the policy documentation. Regrettable, but it's a fact that if the illness is not listed it isn't insured and the policy won't pay out.

The moral is to closely compare the illnesses covered by competing insurance companies (as mentioned above) and buy the one with the most extensive coverage of illnesses. If you don't, sods law will prevail.

How much cover do you need?

Calculating the amount of critical illness cover required can be a little more difficult than life assurance, simply because you don't know the extent of the damage that a critical illness may cause.

It could be that you have a mild stroke and you're back at work within 3 months. Your finances and your lifestyle may not even be affected if you are entitled to receive full salary from your employers.

However, it could be that you suffer a total and permanent disability which will stop you from working forever and you need to spend a lot of money converting your property to provide for your needs.

As its therefore difficult to predict then it may be easier to follow the same principles that we used to calculate the amount of life assurance you require-

1. How much will you need to pay off all debts

2. Identify any income shortfall

3. Take off existing provision

The income shortfall is obviously the variable here that you can't predict so you may want to increase the amount of lump sum to an amount that may provide an 'extra cushion'. Of course, the other thing to consider is cost. As critical illness is more expensive than life assurance (especially if you are a smoker) it may be worth getting quotes for different amounts and choosing the level of cover that is affordable.

Wolf No. 3 - Illness

Official figures show that every year more than 670,000 men aged between 40 and 64 are absent from work for more than six months because of illness. If you are ill, you may be able to get Statutory Sick Pay (SSP) for 28 weeks but this is only £86.70* a week and it has strict eligibility rules. Furthermore, after 28 weeks of illness you must then undergo a test checking your ability to carry out a range of work-related activities such as walking, sitting and using stairs. As you can see, even if you do qualify, benefits are not generous AND they are taxable.

*As of 2013/2014 tax year

Permanent health insurance (or income protection plans as they are sometimes known) differ to critical illness in that the benefit will be paid not on the diagnosis of a specified illness but on a doctor's note stating that you are unable to work due to your illness or injury. This offers a much broader range of potential claims but insurance companies have different definitions of what constitutes a long-term illness. You can be fairly confident that it's not enough just to feel a little bit poorly. Usually to trigger the policy's benefits you must demonstrate that you're unable to follow your usual occupation as a result of sickness or accident.

Some policies insist that you must be unable to do any occupation before benefits are paid - avoid these where possible. They are a licence for insurance companies to make huge profits from your misery because making a valid claim is much harder.

When calculating the amount of cover required from an income protection plan you need to take into account the following-

How much income will you need to cover your living costs? This will include your mortgages (unless it's already covered by a separate accident and sickness policy), your bills, your food etc. Then establish what benefits, if any, your employer provides in terms of sick pay. If your company does provide a group health insurance scheme make sure you join that before considering taking out a personal plan as premiums will usually be much cheaper than if you bought the identical cover yourself, if not free. If they don't provide any benefits than you will need to work on the current rates of statutory sick pay (SSP).

Income Protection Calculation

	£
Monthly living costs	
Minus employer sick pay (or SSP)	
= Income shortfall	

One important point to mention when calculating the level of cover on a permanent health insurance policy is that there are government limits that restrict income protection payments. Many insurance companies will only allow you to protect 55-65% of your income. This is to ensure that people are sufficiently motivated to return to employment. Some companies will only cover up to 50% of income.

Here's an example. Fred earns £30,000 per year and will get full pay for 3 months from his employer if he's unable to work, after which he gets nothing from his employer so will receive SSP of £86.70 for the next 15 weeks. He's worked out that he needs a minimum of £15,000 just to cover his basic expenses, which is £288 per week. Obviously, his statutory sick pay will only cover a small portion of this so he needs approximately £200 per week cover now.

Fred then needs to get a quote for £200 per week or £10,400 per year (the shortfall) so we can decide if he wants to pay this premium to protect him.

There are also other products on the market that pay for a shorter period in time. Accident and sickness policies generally pay benefits for a period of 1-2 years. These can often work out cheaper than permanent health insurance policies as the long term risk for the insurance company is less. Many of these policies also don't rate your policy in terms of profession (you try getting a quote if you're a roofer and then compare it to someone who sits in an office doing admin work – it's a big difference!) However, many of the providers of these types of plans restrict the purchase to when you're taking out a loan or a mortgage.

In short I would get quotes for both. If you understand the advantages and disadvantages of each and can compare the premiums for both you will be able to make a better decision.

Wolf No. 4 - Redundancy

Writing this section in 2012/2013 the term 'redundancy' is being used quite a lot in the news at the moment (actually it's been used quite a lot for the last few years!!). The emergency budget from the coalition government has even got the public sector frightened for their jobs by stating that 80% of the deficit will be raised by cuts in expenses rather than raising taxes. The Labour force survey stated that 939,000 people were made redundant in 2009 and, in the first quarter of 2010 there were another 177,000. Protecting your essential outgoings against this threat would be a good idea for people in this situation.

There are policies available in the market place specifically to cover this problem. The slight problem is that many of these policies, like the accident and sickness policies mentioned above, are aimed at clients who are at the point of either buying a home or re-mortgaging a home. To take out a policy whilst you're already in a mortgage is a little more difficult as there are less providers in the market place and the premiums are higher. They will also be a little more stringent with the questions on their application forms to avoid people taking out insurance just after they've heard about redundancies at their firm.

Generally, these premiums are charged at a rate of £2-5 per month for every £100 of monthly benefit. So, if we use the £3 figure as an example, then £500 per month of redundancy cover will cost £15. These plans will usually pay out the benefit for 12-24 months so you will have to get a job before the policy stops paying the benefits.

The one good thing about redundancy is that you may be entitled to a redundancy payment from your employer if you have worked there for more than 2 years. If this is the case then you can factor this payment into your protection needs too.

The minimum legal payment an employer must make when making staff redundant is as follows:-

0.5 week's pay for each full year of service where your age was under 22

One week's pay for each full year of service where your age was 22 or above, but under 41

1.5 week's pay for each full year of service where your age was 41 or above

In practice, many employers will opt to pay more. Some will pay two weeks per year with the most generous considering three weeks.

Other areas of Protection

There are also others areas of protection that people should consider based on their circumstances. Writing a will or putting policies in trust will give you peace of mind that the benefits will go to the right places. Using trusts (or other tax efficient methods) can also help your beneficiaries protect against paying a 40% tax bill on the amount of your estate above the inheritance tax threshold.

Making a lasting power of attorney with a solicitor ensures your assets can be managed by someone you trust should you be unable to manage your own affairs.

It's also worth making sure your home and contents are adequately covered together with other items that you consider valuable.

Final Points

I have given you some basic methods on how to calculate the levels of cover you need however, there are several online tools to calculate the amount of insurance you may need depending on your circumstances. You will usually need to input your debts, household expenditure costs, age and number of children, net income etc and then it will produce a suggested amount of cover for you. Just type in 'life assurance calculators' 'income protection calculators' critical illness calculators' etc and you'll find plenty of sites.

Remember, before you start paying any money for protection products make sure you are aware of what benefits, if any, are available from your employer. Some employers will provide up to 4 times your salary to your estate if you die and will pay an income if you are incapacitated. If you have a company pension then there could either be a lump sum available or maybe an income for life for your nominated beneficiary. Notice I say 'your nominated beneficiary' rather than your spouse? I say this because the decision of where this benefit will go is down to the trustees of the pension scheme. Most times it WILL go to your wife but, if you're not married, then I would strongly suggest you ask your pension scheme provider for a 'nomination of beneficiary form'. Completing this will help to ensure the money goes where you want it to go. It's a bit like writing a will for your pension.

Shop around to keep the costs down and get the right cover

We have to remember that insurance is a gamble. You're simply paying your money in return for a pay-out should a disaster occur. If a disaster doesn't occur then you don't get anything back. The key is to make sure you get the right level of cover for a competitive premium.

To make sure you get a competitive premium, shop around. Don't just get a quote from your bank on this stuff as they're usually more expensive than what you can get elsewhere. Go on comparison websites or seek independent advice. The same level of cover can cost significantly more from one provider to another. Likewise, in terms of critical illness, there can be varying amounts of illnesses covered against so you need to make sure you read the small print to make sure you get the most cost effective plan for your money. One good thing about buying insurance is that the policies will still pay commission after the Retail Distribution review so it's unlikely you will have to pay for protection advice via upfront fees so feel free to speak to an independent adviser rather than feel you have to do it yourself to save money.

Prioritise if budget constraints apply

To cover against every potential catastrophe can often be expensive. I often have had clients say they would like to cover against certain wolves but they simply can't afford it. When this happens, prioritise.

Work out which wolf will have the worst consequence and plan for that first. If you have a small family then it may be the death of a bread winner that will have the worst effect. If you are a single person with a large mortgage then a critical illness may be the biggest catastrophe. By prioritising you can at least cover against the biggest threats first.

So, that's the 6th step covered. I appreciate that the theme of protecting against catastrophes is not the most appealing of subjects. However, there is some good news. In the next chapter we will be setting off on our journey and heading for the landmarks on your **lifeline**.

To summarise –

1. Establish which of the wolves you need to protect against.

2. Work out how much you need to maintain your lifestyle should a catastrophe happen

3. Find out the cover you have in place already

4. Shop around to get the most cost effective cover to fill the gap.

5. Prioritise what's most important and cover against what would cause the biggest problem should affordability be an issue.

Now buckle up and turn on the engine. We're about to set off on our journey in chapter 7 and achieve those landmarks along the way by covering the subject of saving.

Chapter 7 –Reaching your Landmarks

Dishonest money dwindles away, but he who gathers money little by little

makes it grow.

~Proverbs 13:11

Or….if you look after the pennies, the pounds look after themselves
~My Mum!

Hooray, at long last we can release the hand break and set off on the journey. It's time to get excited and see what can happen now that you've organised your finances to achieve various purposes. It's now time to start seeing the landmarks become reality as we schedule them into our trip.

There are some fantastic things that you can do on this planet, both for yourself and for others, and it would be a shame to go through it and not experience some of the good things life can offer. If you live in the modern world you're blessed with the opportunity to create opportunities. It's possible to get a job, start a business and give yourself a chance in life to get ahead.

In fact, if you live in the UK, USA or Australia, you're probably wealthy already when you compare yourself to our brothers and sisters in the third world nations.

Saving is simply a way of paying yourself!

The latest world poverty statistics (July 2012) state that half of the world's 6 billion population live on less than $2.50 per day and 80% of the people in the world live on less than $10 per day! So how blessed we are to be even talking about the opportunity of saving.

So whether it's attending your child's university graduation ceremony, taking a balloon ride over the African plains or even giving to the poorer people mentioned above, the important thing is that you review the answers you put down to the questions in chapter 1 and then review the priorities and life stages/events that you placed on your lifeline. Once you've done that we can now start to talk about the exciting aspects of saving towards your goals. So come on, release the hand break, put your foot on the accelerator and let's move forwards towards those landmarks on your timeline.

As mentioned in the introduction, the financial planning process is a journey and your time line is a visual map of that journey. It's a journey that can (and usually will) consist of many twists and turns, many highs and lows. It's a long way, a very long way, maybe 90 years long! With this in mind I think it's fairly acceptable to build in some stops along the way don't you? If we don't, we'll miss some amazing sights.

So, let's just recap on the planning stage we covered in chapter 1 before we launch your savings strategy.

The 7 steps in planning the journey are –

1. Evaluate what's really important

2. Create your *lifeline*

3. Decide on the life stages and events you want to plan for

4. Place them on your *lifeline*

5. Work out the costs

6. Add in likely receipts

7. Prioritise

If you have also analysed your budget (chapter 2) and established how much you can now set aside for your goals we're then ready to put your foot on the accelerator.

One of the main goals when budgeting is to cover all your basic needs, have enough money for some luxuries and still allow for as much money as possible to be available for future goals. This, in my 20+ years experience as a financial planner, is where I see most of the problems occur for households. People don't set aside sufficient monies to save for the future, preferring instead to spend any spare cash on enjoying themselves today.

In 2009 Aegon surveyed 1524 people in the UK aged between 30 and 65 on matters regarding saving for the future. It showed that 25% of 30-40 year olds would reduce pension contributions instead of luxury expenditure if they had budget constraints.

Now don't get me wrong, there is nothing wrong with having the odd take away, meal out, new outfit etc. After all, good financial planning is all about achieving the lifestyle you want today ***and tomorrow.*** What

People don't set aside sufficient monies to save for the future, preferring instead to spend any spare cash on enjoying themselves today.

is a problem, however, is if you're spending £80 per week on takeaways and then moaning you've no money left at the end of the week for your future. Or if you have 3 wardrobes full of 'nothing to wear' and still need the urge to spend all your spare cash on that new outfit with a few quid added on to the Visa to get the matching shoes as well !! What I'm talking about is balance and, as I keep repeating in this book, **balance is the process of achieving a comfortable lifestyle today without depleting your lifestyle tomorrow.**

It's all about balance

"But I might be dead tomorrow", I've heard some people say. Well yeah you're right but there's a higher chance that you won't so remember, live for today BUT plan for tomorrow. Trust me, I'm a financial adviser!!

Let me give you an example of how you can start to plan to achieve things on your timeline by creating a savings plan.

Meet Paul. Paul is a 40 year old male and earns £40,000 per year. This means, after tax and national insurance (as at 2013/14 tax year) he brings home £2497

Live for today.
Plan for tomorrow.

per month. After analysing his expenditure and when he's factored in all his necessities and luxuries such as holidays, Christmas etc. he's established that 'life' costs him £2097 per month. He therefore has £400 per month disposable income that he can use for his future right?

Fortunately Paul has read chapter 1 of this book. He's listed his financial goals, placed them on his *timeline* and then prioritised this from 'most important' to 'least important'. This helped him to establish that retiring at 60 is what's most important to him. After analysing his pensions forecast, it states that he will receive £16,000 per year, or 40% of his current income, when he reaches 60 (if you don't know what percentage of your current salary your pensions are going to provide then don't worry as we will be covering retirement planning in chapter 9).

£16,000 per year works out at £1114 per month, which is a drop of £1360 per month when compared to his current net income.

However, Paul has looked at his expenditure and worked out that, if he receives an income of 60% of what he earns now he will be able to maintain a similar lifestyle when he's 60. This is because approximately 40% of his current expenditure goes on his mortgage, savings and children's expenditure, all of which will end before he retires.

60% of £2474 is £1484 per month. He already has £1114 forecasted so his total shortfall is therefore £370 per month, or £ 4440 per year. However, this shortfall will disappear when he's eligible to receive his state pension (at 68 based on current legislation) so all we need to cover is 8 years shortfall right?

Ok then, looking at the image below, and taking Paul's age into account we can assume that he has 20 years to build up some savings that can cover a shortfall of £4440 per year for 8 years (or £35,520). Paul now needs to work out how much to save per month to achieve a fund of £35,520 in 20 years time.

A really simple way to do this as follows-

TARGET (£35520) divided by no. of years to go (20) divided by 12 months.

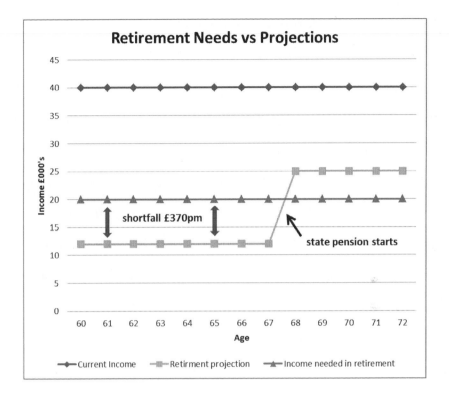

In this example we therefore have the following result:-

£35520 divided by 20 = £2960 divided by 12 = £148

There you go, priority no.1 on the timeline is now sorted! All Paul needs to do is allocate £148 of the £400 per month he has spare to his retirement goal and Bob's your Uncle (as we say in Yorkshire).

WARNING!!! The above example is a very simple formula to help you understand that financial planning is basically just common sense. In fact, once you've set your goals, it just takes a little foresight and a calculator to get the numbers right.

Going back to my journey analogy it's the same as working out how many miles it is to the next landmark and then working out how much fuel you will need based on your cars miles per gallon.

However, if you want to be more specific with regards to the amount of money you need to save then you should really factor in 'the eighth wonder of the world' – compound interest rates!

Compound interest is simply the effect of the interest you have received receiving more interest! In other words, if you had £1000 invested at 5% per year we could assume that, after the first year, you would have £1000 +5%, or £1050. The following

> *Compound interest is 'the effect of the interest you have received receiving more interest'*

year you would receive 5% interest on £1050, which would give you a total of £1102.50 – an extra £2.50p in interest when compared to the first year because your extra £50 is now receiving interest too. The next year you would receive 5% on top of £1102.50, a return of £55.10....and this goes on on and on and on etc. If you multiply this over 20 years you would have £2653.30, with the final years interest being £126.40 – two and a half times the £50 you first received.

For the mathematicians reading this the formula for compound interest rates would look like this...

(Original Amount + Earned Interest) x Interest Rate x Time On Deposit = Total Interest Earned

When you are saving for a future event it's important to factor in compound interest rates as it reduces the amount you need to invest to achieve the same end result. There are calculators and online programs you can use to factor in inflation and different rates of return on your investment in order to get a more realistic requirement of the amounts you need to save. Just go to google and search for 'savings compound interest rate calculators' and you'll find plenty of choice.

These will help you to get a more accurate idea of the amounts you will need to save to reach a certain amount in a certain time frame. In the above example we did for Paul, when factoring a return of 5% compound, it reduces the monthly contribution required from £148 down to £86 – a big difference eh?

However, whilst we have compound interest rates working in your favour, we also have something called inflation working against you! If inflation also runs at 5% per year for 20 years too then it may be better to stick to the £148 payments so they balance each other out.

Now that we have a plan in place to achieve Paul's most important goal we can now move onto his second highest priority and start doing the same calculations for goal no.2. Paul now has £252 left to apply to this as we've already used £148 of his £400 disposable income for goal no. 1 (or £314 if we assume 5% compound returns and use the figure of £86 instead).

Hopefully you will now get the idea that it's quite easy to create a targeted savings plan. If so, then stop reading this book for a second and spend a little time analysing YOUR goals, prioritising them and then revisiting YOUR budget to see what disposable income YOU can allocate to these goals. Go on, do it now....reading further will not help you apply any of these principles and it's the application that will get you the results, not the learning! Go on, start at priority no.1 and do what Paul did, then move onto priority no.2 and then repeat it until you've either ticked off all your goals or you run out of disposable income, whichever comes first....

Where to put the savings

When you start a savings programme there are a few things that you need to consider in order to make sure you get the best returns possible on your money within the time frame you've set. This is where a knowledge of how different accounts and products work will be handy. Obviously, in a brief chapter we can't cover every type of savings account or savings product. Neither can I say which is most suitable without knowing your circumstances so I will generalise and give you a basic guide on the range of accounts to use based on the length of time you need to save. A good way to remember this is to use the acronym 'Saving is an ART', where ART stands for **Availability - Risk/Return - Taxation**

1. Availability

If the goal you're planning for is in the near future then there's no point putting money in accounts that penalise you for short term withdrawals.

Saving is an art

Likewise, there's no point putting your money in an account that is easily accessible but pays little or no interest if you can afford to leave it for a longer term.

So, one of the main determinations of where to put your savings will be based on the length of time it will be invested – and obviously this will be determined by when the goal is on your time line.

If you've got your emergency fund sorted then it's highly likely that you will be able to afford to take a longer term view on your savings. However, if you're really cautious and like to see your money in bank or building society accounts then you may be happy to choose funds that have higher rates for leaving the money for the term of the plan. There are always plenty of accounts that run from 3 months to 5 years that offer some reward for leaving your money in for that length of time.

Be warned however. Don't just take your bank's sales pitch into account when choosing the product to save in. Remember that banks advisers only sell their own products and are targeted to sell them. Do your own research first. 5 minutes on the internet is all it takes to find out what the whole market is offering. Sites like www.moneysupermarket.com are perfect for this and can make a big difference to the return you will get.

Below is a chart that can help you analyse which products are the most suitable based on the requirement to access your funds within a certain time frame.

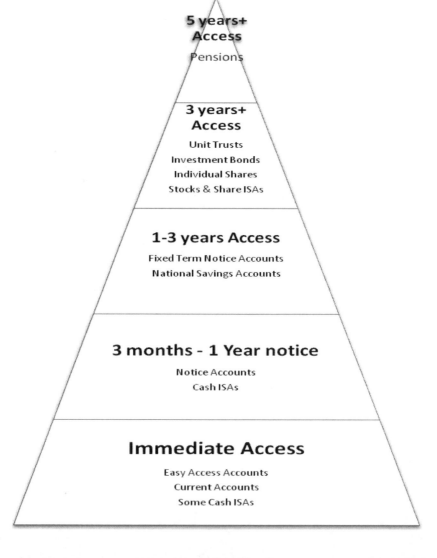

1. Risk/Reward

The next chart is a good indicator of the risk and expected return of

different asset classes (apologies for making you tilt your head)

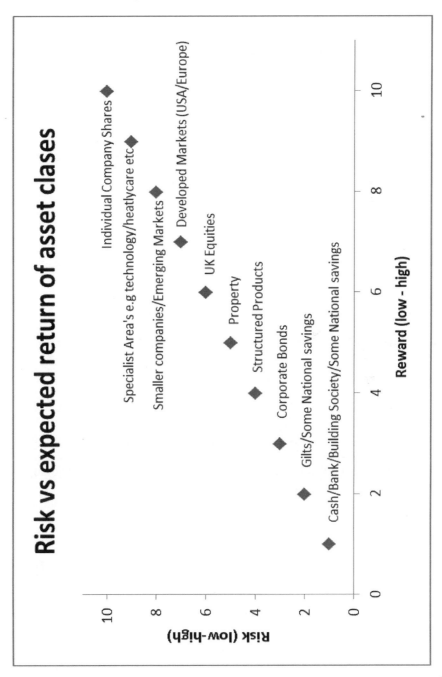

We will cover the risk versus reward issue much more in the next chapter when we deal with the subject of investing but, in the meantime, the previous chart shows where you will see a variety of different products (or asset classes as financial planners call them) that you can use to grow your savings.

The different asset classes are ordered in ascending level of risk with lowest variability of returns to the left and highest to the right.

All investments carry some degree of risk. Generally the rule is "the higher the risk, the higher the potential return," but you need to consider an addition to the rule so that it states the relationship more clearly: "the higher the risk, the higher the potential return, and the less likely it will achieve the higher return."

You need to know what level of risk is attached to the product you intend to use, is your capital exposed and, if so, does it suit the level of risk you are comfortable with?

A balanced savings or investment portfolio will often use a variety of the above products (or asset classes). Cautious portfolio's will have more less volatile sectors on the left of the and less of the 'riskier' funds to the right whilst an adventurous portfolios will be more weighted to the asset classes to the right and less to the left.

Don't worry if you don't fully understand this as we will be going in to more details on 'asset allocation' in the next chapter which deals with investing.

The asset classes you choose in your portfolio may also be determined by the rate of return required. A good adviser will be able to calculate the rate of return required for you to achieve your goal, and then guide you as to how to make up a portfolio that will give you the best chance of achieving it.

For example, if you have quite a large goal but insufficient funds to achieve it then you could opt to increase the risk of the portfolio to attempt to increase the return.

If you have a small goal with considerable funds to allocate to it then you may not need or want to take a risk with your funds if it's not required.

Again, a lot of this will be explained in the next chapter.

2. Taxation

Different products have different taxable benefits. Some products receive tax relief on your contributions i.e. the government will give you some money towards your investment. Some products receive the incentive of tax free growth i.e. no money is taken out of your savings so you receive 100% of the growth and some products are taxable i.e. for every £100 of growth you pay a percentage of it to the government in tax.

For example, a basic rate taxpayer who invests £100 and receives a return of 5% will have a balance of £131.25 if it was invested in a pension, £105 if it was invested in an ISA and £104 if it was invested in a bank account. This is because the £100 contribution to a pension will receive tax relief so the gross contribution will be £125, plus the 5% = £131.25, the £100 into an ISA will not receive tax relief but the £5 growth will be tax free, the £100 into a bank account won't receive tax relief either and the interest of £5 will be taxed at 20%, leaving £104 in the account.

Choosing the right product, therefore, is also a very important part of the savings process. Can you imagine the effect on the above calculation if we took a 20 year term into account? The gap would be massive. To help you, hopefully the image below will give you an indication, as of tax year 2012/2013, of what products you can choose and the appropriate tax situation that applies.

TAXABLE	TAX FREE	TAX FREE & TAX RELIEF
Instant Savings Accounts	Cash ISA's	Pensions
Notice Accounts	Stocks & Share ISAs	Venture Capital Trusts
Some National Savings	Some National Savings	Enterprise Investment schemes
	Unit Trusts	

I did debate if it was beneficial to cover a detailed analysis of the taxation of savings and investment products in this part of the book or whether it would make you lose the will to live! Unable to reach a conclusion I've decided to cover such details, but to place it at the back of the chapter with a 'boring alert'. This, I thought, would allow the ones who are interested in the finer details to learn whilst those that would prefer to skip the intricacies and seek advice from people like me, can now go straight to the next chapter without feeling guilty!

Finally, on the subject of savings, there are just 2 more issues I'd like to make you aware of.

1. Make the most of your personal income allowances

If you have a non-earning spouse, or civil partner, you can switch income-earning investments to help your tax bill. Everyone up to age 65 has a personal allowance of £9,440 in the 2013/14 tax year, rising to £10,500 between the ages of 65 and 74 and £10,660 if you're 75 and over*. This means you can earn this amount without paying any income tax.

2. Use capital gains tax allowances wisely

Everyone can make up to a certain amount of profit each year from selling an investment or property without paying tax. In the 2013/2014 tax year this allowance is £10,900* so think about switching investments to a spouse's or civil partner's name to take advantage of both of your allowances.

*Always check the current personal allowance for the tax year you're in

To summarise-

1. Identify the goals on your *lifeline* and the date you want to achieve it.

2. Prioritise them in order of importance

3. Work out how much it will cost.

4. Work out how much you need to save each week/month/year to achieve that amount.

5. Decide which product to use based on tax, term and amount of risk you're willing to take

Finally, reminding you of what we did in chapter 1 on building your *lifeline,* when you put all this together you might have a *lifeline* that looks something like this now...

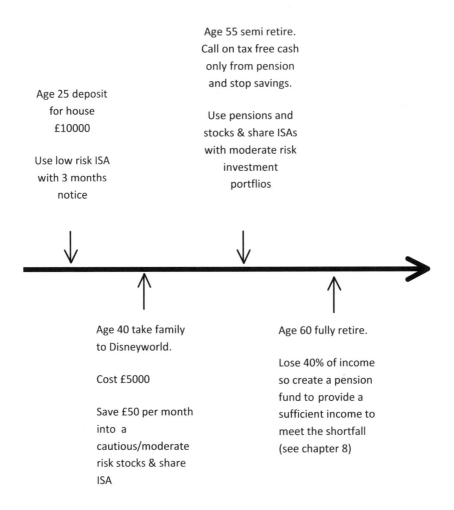

Age 55 semi retire.
Call on tax free cash
only from pension
and stop savings.

Age 25 deposit
for house
£10000

Use pensions and
stocks & share ISAs
with moderate risk
investment
portflios

Use low risk ISA
with 3 months
notice

Age 40 take family
to Disneyworld.

Cost £5000

Save £50 per month
into a
cautious/moderate
risk stocks & share
ISA

Age 60 fully retire.

Lose 40% of income
so create a pension
fund to provide a
sufficient income to
meet the shortfall
(see chapter 8)

As you can see, we have your *lifeline* with your goals and the corresponding dates on it together with the monetary amounts you will need to achieve the goal. We also now have included the products you're going to use that are the most suitable in terms of tax efficiency, availability and risk vs return. It's a simple process of goal -> amount required -> method to create it -> product to use.

At this stage you have a pretty comprehensive financial plan taking shape. Believe me, people who create plans like this will always achieve substantially more than people who just drift through life letting their hard earned cash slip through their fingers.

Go on now, do yours whilst it's fresh in your mind.

Now let's start to speed up your savings and assets growth by covering investing in chapter 8, or 'Turning on the Turbo' as I like to call it.

WARNING – POTENTIAL BORING ALERT!!!

The next few pages are not the most exciting part of the book. (What do you mean neither was the rest ???)

So, here we go.....the following is based on an understanding of current taxation, legislation and HM Revenue & Customs practice as at April 2013, all of which are subject to change without notice. The impact of taxation (and any tax relief) will also depend on individual circumstances.

Bank Accounts

Interest earned in bank accounts is taxable at your highest rate of tax. If you or your partner are non-taxpayers, however, you can avoid the automatic 20% tax deduction on interest by completing form R85 from your bank or product provider or reclaim it using form R40 from HM Revenue & Customs.

Individual Savings Accounts (ISAs)

You pay no personal income tax or capital gains tax on any growth in an ISA, or when you take your money out. You can save up to £11,520 per person in the 2013/14 tax year in an ISA.

If you invest in a stocks and shares ISA, any dividends you receive are paid net, with a 10% tax credit. There is no further tax liability.

National Savings & Investments

NS&I (advertised recently by Lord Sugar on TV) is a government-backed savings institution that allows you to shelter money in a tax-efficient way. Products included in the NS&I brochure are premium bonds, index-linked savings certificates and fixed interest savings certificates. Some are tax free and some are taxable. For more information you can go to the National Savings & Investments website at www.nsandi.com.

Unit Trusts and Open Ended Investment Companies (OEICs)

With a Unit Trust or OEIC your money is pooled with other investors' money and can be invested in a range of sectors and assets such as stocks and shares, bonds or property. Taxation on these products can be complicated as you can receive different types of return such as income from dividends, income from fixed interest funds and there are also capital gains tax implications.

Dividend income from OEICS and unit trusts invested in shares

If your fund is invested in shares then any dividend income that is paid to you (or accumulated within the fund if it is reinvested) carries a 10% tax credit. If you are a basic rate or non- taxpayer, there is no further income tax liability. Higher rate taxpayers have a total liability of 32.5% on dividend income and the tax credit reduces this to 22.5%, while the additional rate taxpayers have a total liability of 42.5% reduced to 32.5% after tax credit is applied.

Interest from fixed interest funds

Any interest paid out from fixed interest funds (these are funds that invest for example in corporate bonds and gilts, or cash) is treated differently to income from funds invested in shares.

Income is paid net of 20% tax. So for example if interest of £100 had been generated, you would receive a net payment of £80.

Taxpayer	Interest paid net of tax	Reclaim tax	Further payment required
Non taxpayer	20%	Yes, you can reclaim the 20% tax paid.	No
Basic rate taxpayer	20%	No you cannot reclaim the tax.	No
Higher rate taxpayer	20%	No you cannot reclaim the tax.	Yes, a further 20% tax payment required.
Additional rate taxpayer	20%	No you cannot reclaim the tax.	Yes, a further 30% tax payment required.

Capital gains tax

No capital gains tax is paid on the growth in your money from the investments held within the fund, but when you sell, you may have to pay capital gains tax.

Bear in mind that you have a personal capital gains tax allowance that can help you limit any potential tax liability. Any gains over this allowance are taxed at 18%, regardless of whether you are an additional, higher or basic rate taxpayer.

Onshore investment bonds

Investment bonds have a different tax treatment from other investments. This can lead to some valuable tax planning opportunities for individuals.

- There is no personal liability to capital gains tax or basic rate income tax on proceeds from your bonds. This is because the fund itself is subject to tax, equivalent to basic rate tax.

- You can withdraw up to 5% each year of the amount you have paid into your bond without paying any immediate tax on it. This allowance is cumulative so any unused part of this 5% limit can be carried forward to future years (although the total cannot be greater than 100% of the amount paid in).

- If you are a higher or additional rate taxpayer now but know that you will become a basic rate taxpayer later (perhaps when you retire for example) then you might consider deferring any withdrawal from the bond (in excess of the accumulated 5% allowances) until that time. If you do this, you will not need to pay tax on any gains from your bond.

Onshore investment bond considerations

Certain events during the lifetime of your bond may trigger a potential income tax liability such as

- death

- Some transfers of legal ownership of part or all of the bond.

- On the maturity of the bond (except whole of life policies).

- On full or final cashing in of your bond.

- If you withdraw more than the cumulative 5% annual allowance. Tax liability is calculated on the amount withdrawn above the 5%.

If you are a higher or additional rate taxpayer or the profit (gain) from your bond takes you into a higher or additional rate tax position as a result of any of the above events then you may have an income tax liability.

As you are presumed to have paid basic rate tax, the amount you would liable for is the difference between the basic rate and higher or additional rate tax.

The events may also affect your eligibility for certain tax credits.

The taxation of life assurance investment bonds held by UK corporate investors changed from 1 April 2008. The bonds fall under different legislation and corporate investors are no longer able to withdraw 5% of their investment each year and defer the tax on this until the bond ends.

Offshore investment bonds

Offshore investment bonds are similar to UK investment bonds above but there is one main difference.

With an onshore bond tax is payable on gains made by the underlying investment, whereas with an offshore bond no income or capital gains tax is payable on the underlying investment. However, there may be an element of withholding tax that cannot be recovered.

The lack of tax on the underlying investment means that potentially it can grow faster than one that is taxed. Note that tax may be payable on a chargeable event at a basic, higher or additional rate tax as appropriate.

Remember that the value of your fund can fluctuate and you may not get back your original investment.

UK shares and taxation

If you own shares directly in a company you may be liable to tax.

- Dividends

Any income (dividends) you receive from your shares carries a 10% tax credit. Higher rate taxpayers have a total liability of 32.5% on dividend income and the tax credit reduces this to 22.5%, while the 50% additional rate taxpayers have a total liability of 42.5% reduced to 32.5% after tax credit is applied.

- Additional rate taxpayer example

Net dividend is £90.

Gross dividend is £100 (includes the 10% tax credit).

Less 42.5% (£42.50) higher rate tax on the gross amount of £100 equals a net dividend of £57.50.

Tax due is £42.50, less 10% tax credit (£10) equals £32.50.

Sales of shares

When you sell shares you may be liable to capital gains tax on any gains you may make. You have a yearly allowance, above which any gains are liable to 18% tax. Special rules apply to working out your gains or losses. - find out more at http://www.hmrc.gov.uk/taxon/buying-shares.htm.

END OF BORING BIT!

Chapter 8 – Turning on the Turbo

Investing is something you do to become wealthy,

not something you do once you become wealthy.

~Me!

OK, so we're on our journey right? We've got our *timeline* with the goals on it (or our journey with the landmarks marked out) and we've started moving towards them, ticking them off as we put the right plans in place to achieve (and enjoy) them.

So here's a question. How would you like to achieve some of them a little quicker? In other words, how would you like to improve the vehicle so it produces its maximum performance? Now I'm not talking about go faster stripes and those tacky blue lights under the chassis, designed to look like you're driving a mobile disco! I'm talking about adding turbo and supercharging the engine so that it improves your vehicle's acceleration. In financial terms I'm talking about investing.

So what's the difference between saving and investing? Well, in terms of concepts I would say very little. To me, the difference is simply this –

Saving money is putting money aside on a regular basis to enable you to reach certain goals. Investing is taking this a step further by dealing with the amounts of money that you have already saved...and making those amounts earn even more.

If investing is done correctly then this could begin to really grow your money faster and start to build wealth, like the effect of a turbo charged engine. You could eventually come to the point where your investments make more than you are contributing each month. However, like the subject of saving, investing is a complicated subject and something that one chapter in a book can only begin to cover. To keep things simple again I am only going to cover some basic investment principles. For more detailed information *I would strongly suggest you seek advice in this area.*

I would relate the DIY investor to someone who likes to fix their own car. Personally, when I have a problem with my car I just take it to the garage, choose to trust them and hope they tell me the cost to repair is minimal. Should they lift the bonnet up to explain what they've done then, to be honest, I'm not really interested. You see, I understand that the mechanics of an engine are fairly complicated and that I'm not competent in fixing them. My focus is more on driving it and using it to get me from A to B!

Well investing is similar. If you're only interested in knowing that the car will get you from A-B then seek advice however, if you do like to develop your own investment portfolio's then feel free to read on and I'll show you how to 'get under the bonnet'.

So, let's look at the basics of an investment process. Again, I apologise if some of the following information gets a little heavy but I prefer to include important information rather than simply skip over issues because they are complicated. But be warned, this could be a heavy chapter!

1. Establish the Purpose

An investment should be working to achieve one of your life events or stages. I often see people that want to invest money but have no real goal or purpose for their money to achieve. Here are just a few questions that need to be asked before you invest:-

- Why am I investing it?

- Does it need to be available at a specific time?

- Does it need to reach a certain figure?

- Is it simply there to grow above the rate of inflation? If so, by how much?

Let me give you an example. A successful financial planner that I know was once called in to see a client who had just sold his business and had £1.3 million to invest for his retirement. The client was a no-nonsense type character who probably knew a thing or two about business but wasn't fully aware of what he really wanted the money to do. Instead he got caught up with the idea of making the best return possible with his cash, thinking that making the most money was the determining factor for his investment outlook.

My friend said the client started the conversation something like this "Mr Adviser I don't want to mess you about or waste my time

Establishing the purpose of your investment will help you to identify the guidelines of your investment portfolio.

because you're the third adviser I've seen. The first adviser reckons he can get me around 11% return on my investment each year and the second adviser thinks he can get me 12%. What can you do?" My friend simply replied "well in that case, I'll get you 13 then!" The client was a little taken aback by this flippant answer so then pressed for an explanation to which my learned friend answered something like this...

"Mr Client, firstly anyone who promises you a return from your investment of 11-12% will need to take a risk with your money to achieve it. Secondly, I think you're missing the point. The first thing you need to do is establish what the investment's purpose is so we can then, and only then, evaluate the returns it needs to accomplish the job." The client then started to open up a little. "Well really what it needs to do is keep me in the lifestyle I've been used to during my working life" he said.

My friend then started to ask about that lifestyle and dig a little deeper doing his own form of fact-finding mission and attempting to uncover how the client would like it to look (he was subtly getting the client to create his *lifeline*).

Finally, the client started to understand that financial planning should ALWAYS precede financial advice and so became open to going into detail about his goal's, his income, expenditure, assets etc so my friend could analyse the role of the £1.3 million in this. Anyway, to cut a long story short, it was established that the client only needed a return of 1% above inflation on the investment for him and his wife to achieve everything they wanted (which involved them spending 3-4 months per year in their holiday home in Tenerife). **In other words, there was no need to take a large risk in order to achieve the goals on their *lifeline*.**

What my friend said next hits the real point and ethos of good financial planning. He said "Mr Client, if you're priority is to take the necessary risks to achieve 11-12% per annum then go for it and may I wish you the best of luck. However, we have established that a return of 1% above inflation is all that is required for you to live the life you want without running out of money, and we can achieve that with virtually no risk to your capital. All I have to ask you is this. When you're sat on the beach watching the sunset in Tenerife would you want to be enjoying the moment and taking pleasure in what you have achieved or would you want to be worrying if your adviser is taking the right risks with your money to deliver the 11% returns you *think* you need?"

Needless to say, the client created a very cautious investment portfolio with my friend. No doubt, he had a less stressful retirement too.

So, rule number 1 on investing is to establish the 'why, when and the what for'. Then you will have an idea of the level of risk you may need to take to achieve it. If it can be achieved without risk then why bother investing in a speculative fund? If you won a million pounds on the lottery would you go out and buy 1 million tickets the following week to try and win it again? Probably not! If you won a million pounds in Vegas on the roulette table how many of you would be tempted to put it all on red or black to try and double it again? Not me pal, I'd be flying home with a million! (Well maybe a bit less than a million after I'd upgraded to a penthouse suite for the rest of my stay).

2. Establish your 'attitude to risk'.

Following on from the story above the second thing you need to do is find out the level of risk you feel comfortable with when investing money. But you might ask what exactly risk is? Well I like Warren Buffet's description best. "Risk comes from not knowing what you're doing." In other words knowledge is power and the more you learn the less the risk - which is why I stated at the beginning of this step that this is an area I would suggest that you seek advice in, unless you really know what you're doing.

A good example of this is crossing a road. For you and I there's probably little risk when crossing a road as we know to

A good portfolio should attempt to create the highest return for the lowest risk that you're comfortable taking.

look right then left plus we can understand distance and we can judge speed so we can assess whether it's safe to cross or not. Now, put a 2 year old in the same situation and ask them to cross the road! Lo and behold, you have a whole new situation. **Because they don't know what to do like you or I do, RISK enters the scenario.** In fact, how many of you have been in a country where they drive on the opposite side of the road and needed to walk across a dual carriageway? It's amazing how we really have to stop and think which way the cars are coming isn't it?

The way to determine your comfortable level of investment risk will usually involve completing some form of 'attitude to risk' questionnaire. Some are fairly basic and will simply ask you to give a number between 1

Risk comes from not knowing what you're doing.
~Warren Buffet

and 10, with 1 being no risk and 10 being very high risk. But some are far more sophisticated and will help you explore and uncover various emotions that a gain or loss of money will have for you. A good website that I can recommend is http://www.riskprofiling.com/yourrisktolerance. This allows you to do your own risk profile in the demo section and receive a report that compares you to 'the norm'.

Once you know the purpose for your investment and your own risk profile you can then start to build your investment portfolio around it. **The purpose of building a portfolio is to attempt to create the highest possibility of maximising returns within the level of risk you are willing to take with your money - in order to give you the best chance of achieving your goals.**

3. Diversify your assets.

When building a portfolio for non-professional investors the golden rule is to diversify - or in other words "don't put all your eggs in one basket"! When creating an investment portfolio there are many different 'asset classes' you can use to invest in, the main 4 being cash, fixed interest, property and equities (stocks and shares). It's fairly common knowledge that some investments are riskier than others and it's also well known that different investment classes perform differently in different economic climates.

It's important to understand therefore how these different asset classes work so you can make sure you use the most suitable ones for the job, and in the right proportion.

If your investment needs to grow at a high rate and your attitude to risk is adventurous then you may want to put more of your money in to asset classes where there is a chance of higher growth, such as equities and less in the more cautious sectors, such as cash. Equities have a history of outperforming cash over the long term but they are also more volatile (meaning that your money could both rise and fall more sharply).

It's kind of like making a curry. You have various ingredients, some mild and some spicy. If you like a korma then you will probably have more mild ingredients than spicy ones but if you like a vindaloo then you will have a higher concentration of the hot spices. Now there's nothing wrong with a chicken korma, neither is there anything wrong with a chicken vindaloo. The problem arises when someone who likes a korma ends up with a vindaloo! (I know because I've been there, I felt as if my tongue had been temporarily numbed and I'd got a major bout of hay fever!!! Still that's what mates are for eh? - telling the waiter that you like your food hot when you've nipped to the gents!)

Putting different amounts of money into different asset classes is called **asset allocation** and plays a very large factor in the variability of a portfolio's return (variability meaning the different extremes in the rise and fall of an investments value). In fact various studies over the last 20 years or so have shown that asset allocation can be responsible for between 80-93% of the performance variability, with the remainder being down to individual stock selection, market timing or other factors.

How hot would you like your investment?

There have been other studies on the benefits of diversification which concluded that, quite surprisingly, diversification not only reduces risk but it can also increase returns. Harry Markowitz won a Nobel Prize for his creation of something called the 'modern portfolio theory' which explained the concept that the assets in an investment portfolio cannot be selected individually for their own merits. Rather, it is important to consider how each asset changes in price relative to how every other asset in the portfolio changes in price. In other words, if one asset class goes up what do the other asset classes do to react? The way that investments react to one another is

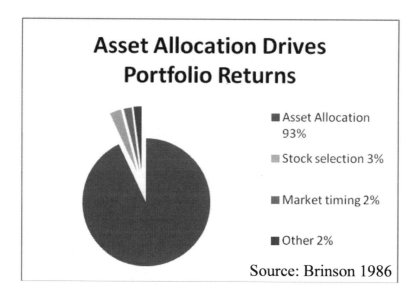

known as correlation.

Historically equities, fixed interest, bonds and cash have not been correlated to one another. What this means is when equities make positive returns, it has been shown that bonds will often make neutral or negative returns. Asset classes with low correlation to each other are good choices for the diversified portfolio as each can perform independently of one another.

Markowitz's Nobel Prize winning theory proved that lower risk and higher risk-adjusted returns can be achieved through investing in non-correlated investments, the lower the correlation (such as ice cream versus umbrella's) then the greater the diversification benefit.

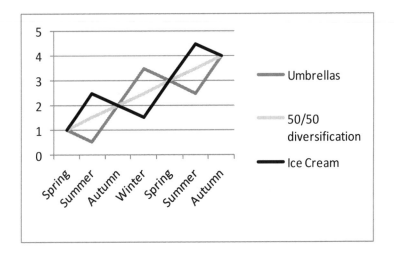

Take a look at the chart above to understand how different assets behave in different ways. The dark line is the returns from a company that sells ice cream. As can be expected the sales increase through spring to a peak in summer but then decrease through autumn to a low in the winter. The grey line is the return from a company that sells umbrellas. Here sales are low in the summer but reach a peak in the winter (unless you live in the UK when you need them all year round!)

The middle line is an equal mix of these two shareholdings, so it's diversified by investing half in each investment.

As you can see from the end result on the chart, it is possible to achieve a similar return by investing 50/50 into both companies over a long period of time BUT you don't experience the ups and downs associated with having just one company. This is the basis of the modern portfolio theory. It also introduces the concept of correlation and non-correlation.

Taking this into a more realistic diversification have a close look at the next image. This is an analysis, done by Frontier Capital Management, of how different portfolios would have compared to each other if invested from January 1991 to July 2008. Here we see the improvements in both the return and the risk from an investment based 100% into UK equities to a portfolio that includes several asset classes in different geographical regions.

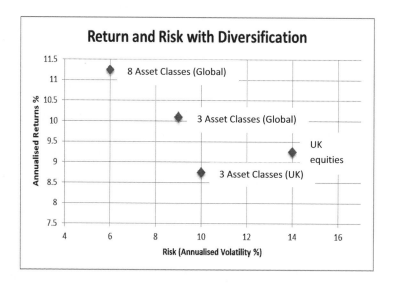

This chart shows that, if you had invested all your money in the UK stock market, you would have received an average return of just above 9% per annum and the volatility (the measurement of the ups and downs in a portfolio) would have been around 14%. However, if you would have spread the money around 8 different asset classes on a global basis you would have received an annual return of over 11% and, wait for it - you would have more than halved the volatility to under 7%. The key, therefore to getting a suitable investment portfolio is making sure you get the right asset allocation according to the level of risk.

The next chart shows a visual image of this concept in a different type of graph. This time the graph is tracking the volatility year on year.

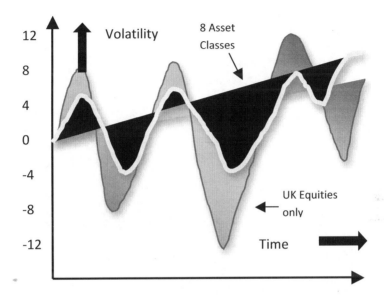

You may notice that the peaks from the UK Equities fund are higher at times than the globally invested fund but overall the return is lower due to the greater drops.

Now I know what some people think...surely it's better to invest in UK Equities and just take the money out during the peaks and then re-invest it at the bottom of the trough? Well actually you're right, that would be fantastic. The problem is this – how will you know when you're at the top of a peak? If you are able to predict this without failure give me your contact details and I will invest all my money with you!

Also, what if you're at the top of the peak but it's not time to take the money out? For example, what if you reach the top of a peak when you're 59 but you don't want to retire until 60? That's a problem now as, at age 60, a volatile fund could fall well away from its peak in 12 months.

So, hopefully these 2 examples will have explained the importance of diversification. Now let's look at how you can do it within an investment portfolio.

4. Understand the different asset classes and their relative risk vs return

Below is another chart that introduces the many different asset classes together with their place on the risk/volatility ladder. The chart shows the maximum gains and losses for each fund sector measured over rolling quarters. It is ordered in ascending level of risk, with lowest variability in returns to the left and highest to the right.

When building an investment portfolio, if you are cautious then you will populate your portfolio with more of the lower risk assets such as cash and fixed interest. If you are speculative then you will buy more of the funds to the right such as equities. This is what I meant earlier when I used the curry example. Spicy ingredients = vindaloo. Speculative funds= volatile portfolio. It's a similar thing.

A good financial adviser will understand how to help you to put these ingredients together based on the results of your risk profile questionnaire just like a good chef will know how to make a korma, a madras or a vindaloo.

However, there are also funds available that you can choose that have these type of assets ready mixed, they're the equivalent of the ready made curries that you find in the supermarkets. They're called managed funds or multi-fund and/or multi-manager funds. You can purchase these off the shelf, usually with the titles of cautious, balanced or adventurous and they have the above assets already diversified to suit.

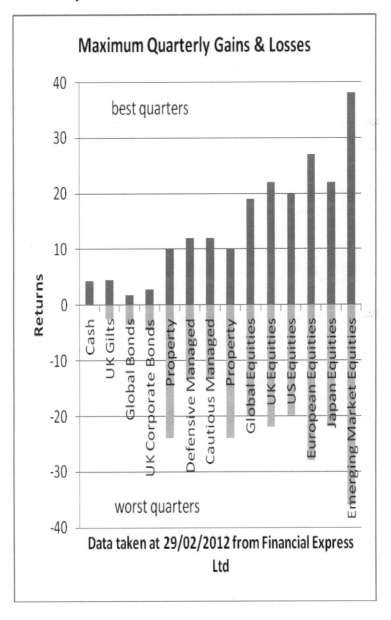

For example, a cautious managed fund may have the following asset allocation-

Fund	% Invested
Cash	5
UK Fixed Interest	21
Global Fixed Interest	20
Property	20
UK Equities	12
US Equities	8
European Equities	4
Global Developed Markets	5
Japan Equities	2
Hedge Funds	2
Emerging Markets	1
TOTAL	100

And an adventurous managed fund will have the following asset allocation-

Fund	% Invested
Cash	1
UK Fixed Interest	7
Global Fixed Interest	6
Property	10
UK Equities	25
US Equities	22
European Equities	8
Global Developed Markets	10
Japan Equities	3
Hedge Funds	5
Emerging Markets	3
TOTAL	100

As you can see the amount invested in the riskier asset classes increases and the amount in the more cautious asset classes decreases in the adventurous portfolio.

Creating your initial asset allocation at the start of your investment is known as **strategic asset allocation.** It's effectively the 'base policy mix' based on the principles of Markowitz's Nobel Prize winning dissertation mentioned earlier. One thing to remember however is that, as your investment starts to feel the effects of the markets, some of your asset classes will grow better than others. This means that you won't keep the same asset allocation. This is where rebalancing comes in. Rebalancing is a process where assets are sold and bought in order to bring the asset allocation back to its original state. I won't go into too much detail now as I will touch upon it in section 8 of the investment process, review and rebalance.

However, as well as strategic asset allocation there is also something called **tactical asset allocation**.

The objective of tactical asset allocation is to alter the amount of funds you have in the different asset classes to try and get an additional return by trying to take advantage of short and intermediate term market views. A tactical allocation process attempts to capture these opportunities (or inefficiencies) by increasing the exposure to the asset classes they feel are good buys and decreasing the allocation to asset classes they're not confident about.

A good way of explaining this is to compare it to the game of squash (or racquet ball). Anyone who's played squash will know that the best place to stand on the court is on the 'T'. This is because you are centrally positioned to return most of the shots your opponent will play against you. In other words, you can react to most situations easier.

You occasionally will move away from the 'T' if you feel confident that your opponent is going to play a particular shot. For example, if he/she looks like they're going to play a drop shot to the front of the court then you might move forward from the 'T' to be able to reach it. If you feel they're going to hit it to the back of the court then you might step back a bit. However, always remember that 'calling' their shot obviously leaves you more exposed in other areas of the court.

Well that's similar to how strategic and tactical asset allocation works. Strategic asset allocation is standing on the 'T'. Tactical asset allocation is standing where you think the market will place its shots. Tactical asset allocation can therefore be more risky if you don't know how to assess the markets and the economy, but it can potentially be more rewarding if you do know how things like economic cycles work. I must admit that, if you do know how to tactically allocate your assets based on the economic cycles or circumstances of the day, then what are you doing reading this book? It's not meant for you! (that's a compliment by the way Mr/Mrs savvy investor).

A word of warning though...tactical asset allocation can increase the risk if you don't know what you're doing! Get it wrong and it can affect the performance over time. Remember the words of Warren Buffet "risk comes from not knowing what you're doing".

5. Choose your Investment Style

OK, let's have a quick recap on how to invest and 'turbo charge' your money. Firstly, you've established the purpose of the investment and hopefully attached it to one of the goals on your timeline. You've then completed a risk questionnaire and/or decided on the level of risk you want to take with this investment. This has now helped you to create a portfolio with a diverse range of asset classes that suit the level of risk you're comfortable taking. The next stage in the investment process is to choose your preferred investment style.

Investment managers (or investment funds) use a variety of styles to attempt to grow your money. They may be a 'value' investor and look for cheap stocks that are out of favour or are at the low end of their business cycle. They could be a 'growth' investor and spend their time looking for companies who are planning to grow in excess of their competition or market average.

They could be a 'small cap' investor who believe that smaller is better due to the fast turnarounds smaller companies can achieve or they could be 'large cap' fans, believing that big companies are more robust and secure. When you invest in funds many of these choices are made by the investment fund managers and so you have little control. However, one choice you can make which strongly sets out the investment criteria a fund manager will stick to is the choice of 'Active versus Passive' investing.

Active Investment is based on the belief that markets can be beaten by taking advantage of irregularities that occur whilst **Passive Investment** managers believe that it is consistently difficult to beat the market.

If you imagine that your investment portfolio is a pie, and the pie is cut into pieces with each piece being a different asset class like the next graph....

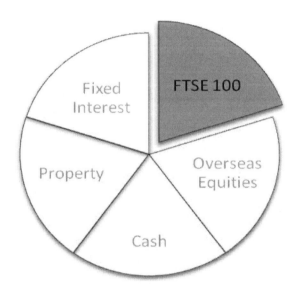

If we look at the slice of the pie that is invested in UK equities you will find that its ingredients will be made up of UK based companies. It could be the FTSE100, which is an index composed of the 100 largest companies listed on the London Stock Exchange (LSE), the FTSE 250 (the top 250 companies on the LSE) or the FTSE all Share. OK, so let's imagine that it's the FTSE100 for one moment (the top 500 companies). If you chose the passive route then you will simply invest into those top 100 companies in a way that replicates the percentage holding the FTSE has.

The top 10 firms in the FTSE (as at February 2012) are BP PLC, HSBC holdings, Vodafone, Glaxosmithkline, Royal Dutch, Shell-A, Royal Bank of Scotland, Royal Dutch Shell -B, Astrazeneca, Barclays, HBOS

Therefore you will buy something that replicates the percentage holding in these companies.

Now if you bought an actively managed fund then you are giving some freedom to a fund manager to decide if he wants to invest in this list of 100 companies with the same weighting or not.

He may decide that several of the FTSE100 companies are not worth investing in to the same degree so he may re direct his investment to other companies (in the same UK sector of course) that he feels have stronger growth potential. His job is effectively to try and sort the winners from the losers and make up a portfolio that's designed to beat the index. This is the main argument on behalf the active manager. They believe they can read the signs and follow the trends that they feel will influence returns, and react accordingly. To try and outperform the market is something called 'seeking alpha' and a fund manager that achieves this regularly will start to get a good reputation in the city.

The potential downside of having an actively managed portfolio is that these guys need paying and so it adds a cost to your investment portfolio.... even if they don't beat the market.

The argument, therefore, is how can you spot the investment managers that regularly outperform the market so you know you're getting your 'alpha'? Well you can analyse the active fund managers by using companies like Morningstar and Standard & Poors. These companies conduct to face interviews with fund managers to give a rating based on their investment style and future strategies. These can be a good starting point to discovering the better funds but they've been wrong in the past, so don't hang your hat on them.

It can be argued that some areas of investment are better suited to active rather than passive management. Property funds, for example, buy commercial properties and pay returns based on rental income and increases in capital value of the properties. A tracker fund simply cannot do this and it may be valuable to invest in an actively managed property fund. Also, an active manager might also be useful in more specialised areas such as technology, healthcare, smaller companies or emerging markets like China. Sometimes having an expert or specialist knowledge in these areas can help fund managers seek out value.

In the more developed markets there's so much information available now on the financial health of companies that it can be argued that active managers find it harder to seek out that 'special information' about a company's future. This availability of information is known as 'market efficiency' – or the efficient market hypothesis if you want to go all posh!

The 'active versus passive' debate has continued for some time now and, no doubt, will continue well into the future. Without being a 100% advocate of either (I like to offer and discuss both strategies with clients and establish which is most suitable based on their requirements here).

Here is a brief table of the advantages and disadvantages of both. Hopefully this will help to encapsulate the main points for both sides of the argument and will help you to gain an understanding of which approach may suit you best.

Passive Management Advantages	Passive Management Disadvantages
Low operating expenses and fees No action required as there is no decision making required by the fund manager or investor.	The performance is dictated by an index. Investors must be satisfied with market returns because that is the best any index fund can achieve. There is a lack of control as managers cannot take action. Index managers are usually unable to move out of stocks if the manager thinks stocks are going to decline. Your portfolio will still buy stocks of companies that may be difficulty because a computer buys what's in the market with no individual analysis.

Active Management Advantages	Active Management Disadvantages
Expert analysis means managers can make informed decisions based on experience and market trends. Possibility of returns higher than the index. Defensive measures available as managers make the necessary changes if they believe there will be a downturn.	Higher fees and operating expenses. Mistakes may happen as there is always the risk that a manager may make a wrong decision that could reduce returns. Style issues may interfere with performance as a managers style may be in or out of favour with the market. Even if they don't beat the market, you still pay them

Get off the fence Brian and tell us what to do!

When having these type of discussions with clients who aren't experienced investors I regularly get asked "what would you do"? Ok, so here's my opinion. First of all I feel that the rate of return required has a big impact on which investment style to choose. If it transpires that a client doesn't need a great rate of return to achieve his goal then I would argue that there's no need to pay extra to active fund managers when it's highly likely that an average market index return will do the job.

If, on the other hand, a high rate or return is required then choosing actively managed funds/fund managers with good track records may be worth pursuing. The challenge is making sure you find them in the first place and then, even more importantly, make sure you monitor their progress against their benchmark.

If you look at the following diagram this is a chart that has analysed fund managers who were in the top and bottom quartiles of the US 'large cap' equity managers (like the FTSE but in the States) during 2000 – 2004 and then tracked them over the following 5 year period from 2004 - 2009. You will see that the variability in the performance is quite high with only 23% of fund managers who were in the top quartile during 2000 – 2004 staying in the top quartile from 2004 – 2009. Interestingly, 9% of bottom quartile managers in 2004 – 2009 ended up being top quartile performers in 2004 – 2009.

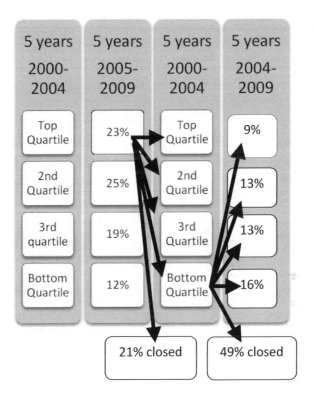

This is the danger in picking 'recommended fund or recommended manager of the month' and then not monitoring the performance. As a sports fan I liken it to watching the football league tables and the performance of the teams. Take a look at the final positions of the football premiership in the 2006-7 season and you will see a similar pattern.

Now we can see a few obvious names here in the top 5 (the ones that stay in the top quartile regularly) but if these football clubs represented investment funds that you had bought in 2006 where would you be now? What if you'd put all your money in Portsmouth, Blackburn, Middlesbrough and Sheffield United?

Team	Played	Won	Drew	Lost	Points
Manchester Utd	38	28	5	5	89
Chelsea	38	24	11	3	83
Liverpool	38	20	8	10	68
Arsenal	38	19	11	8	68
Tott'm Hotspur	38	17	9	12	60
Everton	38	15	13	10	58
Bolton Wndrs	38	16	8	14	56
Reading	38	16	7	15	55
Portsmouth	38	14	12	12	54
Blackburn Rvs	38	15	7	16	52
Aston Villa	38	11	17	10	50
Middlesbrough	38	12	10	16	46
Newcastle Utd	38	11	10	17	43
Manchester City	38	11	9	18	42
West Ham Utd	38	12	5	21	41
Fulham	38	8	15	15	39
Wigan Athletic	38	10	8	20	38
Sheffield United	38	10	8	20	38
Charlton Ath	38	8	10	20	34
Watford	38	5	13	20	28

On the other side what if you would have invested in Manchester City, a team that were just above the relegation zone at that time? You get the picture?

You see football team managers and fund managers have a lot in common in the fact that the assets (or players) they buy, combined with how they perform together on the pitch (correlation) and the success of the tactics (investment style) determines the performance and thus the end result, whether it be league position or investment growth.

By the way, as a Liverpool fan I'm sure you'll understand my reasons for not putting the current tables up. We're languishing in the relegation zone at present and the pain of typing it was just too much for a grown man to bear!*

(*update - just doing some last minute corrections and would like to say the league position has improved somewhat over the last 3 months - relief!)

6. Select the right Tax Wrapper

Tax Wrapper is simply another name for product. The most popular products used for investing clients money are ISA's, Unit Trusts (or OEICS), Bonds (both onshore and offshore) and Pensions. There are also other products you can use such as direct investment in shares, Enterprise Investment Schemes and Venture Capital Trusts etc but I just feel these are outside the scope of a basic chapter on investing as they're specialised products and potentially more suited to wealthier investors or those with a greater appetite for investment risk.

Choosing the most suitable tax wrapper is an important part of the investment process as it will determine the level of tax your product will pay and/or the level of tax incentives it will receive. It is also an important decision based on the taxation position of the investor. An inefficient tax wrapper simply means giving part of the investment return to the government when it's simply not necessary.

Paul Kennedy, Head of Tax and Trust Planning at Fidelity International, says: "It is a simple fact that the choice of tax wrapper affects what goes back into the client's pocket. It's such a shame that hours can be spent in selecting the right assets and funds with the client to then be 'robbed' of some of that underlying investment return through poor tax planning".

He has also done an analysis which shows that it was possible (when the 50% tax rate upon us last year) to get a return of 161% more on one wrapper compared to another. This is staggering when you consider it's exactly the same fund, the same manager, the same performance and that difference arises solely because of the tax wrapper.

In the previous chapter I touched upon the taxation of savings products and gave some guidance on the 'ART' of saving. The concept of ART – Availability, Risk and Trust – is technically even more important when investing as you could be dealing with higher amounts of money. It may be worth just having a quick look at the info in chapter 7 rather than repeating myself here.

7. Select a Suitable Provider

Selecting the right manager, company or investment house is the next factor in a comprehensive investment process. Going back to the comparison of investment managers to football managers, choosing the right provider is like investing in the right club. You need to look at the overall size and strength of the club, the quality of the players and the performance in recent times. When analysing factors that determine which funds, companies and investment managers to invest in then you need to look at the following:-

Company Strength – is the company in a strong financial position?

Past Performance (thought this is no guarantee of future performance)

Charges – what are the total charges for the product, the funds, the adviser service charge etc?

Again, this is where the help of a professional will help, although much of this information is freely available online these days. Sites like www.trustnet. com are great for getting information on charges, funds and fund performance. There are also companies such as Standard and Poor's, who provide credit ratings and opinions on the general creditworthiness of insurance companies.

Using tools like this may take time getting used to you but 'knowledge is power' as they say. It's also far more reliable than listening to your mate in the pub! You know the one, the guy who knows everything about everything!

8. Review and Rebalance

Finally, once you have made the investment please don't think that's it for life. It's vital to keep an eye on both the performance of the investment as well as the performance of the individual asset classes/funds within the investment. Initially you should review your performance against some set criteria, say inflation or a specific target you want to achieve at a specific date. This helps to establish whether you're investment is doing its job. It may also be a good idea to compare it with its peers or similar funds in the same sector.

I would suggest that you review your investment at least annually and maybe quarterly for funds that are of a larger nature. This stops your investment 'drifting' should things not go well in the portfolio and allows you to make necessary changes early.

Monitoring your performance towards your goal is also a great way of ensuring any issues are dealt with as early as possible. Ever had a letter from the insurance company stating that your endowment is 'at risk of a shortfall'? You know the ones where it was supposed to pay you £50000 but it looks like it's only going to give you £40000?

Well there's not much you can do about it if you get that letter 12 months before it's due to mature is there? . However, if you get one of these letters with 15 years to go then it gives you plenty of time to make some changes so you don't have £10000 to find in a short space of time. In fact, if you make some positive changes to gain extra performance then there's chance that you could make that extra £10000 over 15 years, so you don't have to put your hand in your pocket.

You could set up a simple excel graph like this that you can use to chart your progress against the original target and so monitor its progress. Each time frame could be a 12 month period with the starting point of the investment ending at the required amount in the correct time frame. Here's an example:-

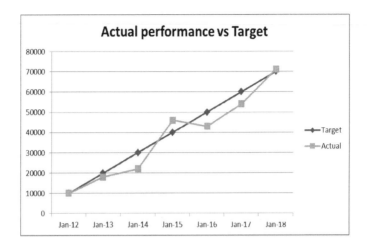

Another suggestion would be to monitor the performance of the individual

asset classes so that they don't get out of balance. For example, let's say

you have a portfolio that suits your attitude to risk and contains 25% cash,

25% fixed interest, 25% property and 25% equities at the beginning of the

investment. Now we know from the points made earlier that equities are more

volatile than cash right? Well, let's assume that the markets are having a good

time and so 1 year later the portfolio looks like this – 15% cash, 15% fixed

interest, 30% property and 40% equities. We now have a situation where the

equity (or riskier) content is higher and the cash (least risky) content is lower.

Technically, this portfolio is now out of line with your original attitude to risk

as it's more exposed to the ups and downs of the equity markets.

Well this is where rebalancing (mentioned in section 4 on asset allocation)

comes in handy.

Assuming you want to stick to your original level of risk then a good idea

would be to sell the equities to reduce back to a 25% exposure and switch it

into cash so that can be brought back up to 25%. The same can be done with the property and fixed interest funds so that the portfolio is back to a 25% split across the board.

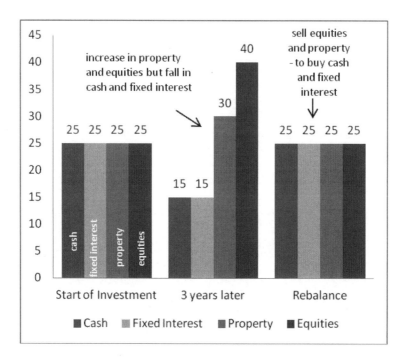

What's the benefit of this? Well the basic argument is that you are selling what's grown (and coining the profit) to buy what's dropped. Or in other words - selling high and buying low. The other argument is that it stops your portfolio from becoming unbalanced to your attitude to risk over time.

Rebalancing can be done in different ways. You can do it on a specific date each year, you can do it when a certain asset class reaches a certain percentage of the investment, you can do it by buying the lower valued funds with new money or you can simply sell and buy as explained above.

Either way, reviewing your investments performance against its pre agreed criteria together with rebalancing as and when necessary should mean that your portfolio has a better job of fulfilling its purpose than just leaving it until maturity to 'see how it does'.

There is no overwhelming evidence that rebalancing improves performance over time but it can't be denied that it will help to keep the risk of the portfolio in line with its initial allocation.

So, as you can see investing is a complicated game and, in my opinion, something that most people should only get involved in with the help of a professional. I've only really skimmed the surface here, preferring to give an overview of some of the factors to consider, rather than an in depth analysis of each point. Ideally, if you're not an experienced investor and want to get in the game then let someone else guide you – just like you'd hold a 2 year olds hand if you want to cross a busy road!

However, if you do want to create your own investment portfolio and don't want the advice of an expert then the biggest advice I can give you is **LEARN THE GAME.** Don't buy based on what your mate in the pub is bragging about because he may have just been fortunate with his timing. And also, don't enter the investment market for the short term. Investing is a long term plan for the masses and only short term for the professionals, and even they get it wrong quite often too!

As mentioned at the beginning of this chapter, I'm not saying this chapter is all encompassing when it comes to the subject of investing. Hopefully, you'll find that it's robust enough to cope with most investor's demands yet simple enough to understand for the novice. For those that do want to go it alone you may find you want to add different stages or criteria into the process, depending on the type of portfolio you're creating. On the other hand, if this chapter has helped you to realise that it may be best to seek guidance when investing money then I suppose it's also done its job.

To summarise-

1. Establish the purpose of the investment

2. Establish your attitude to risk

3. Diversify your assets correctly

4. Choose the style of how you want your investments managed

5. Choose the product (or most efficient tax wrapper)

6. Choose a suitable provider in terms of charges, financial strength and history of performance

7. Review and rebalance

Now onto the subject of planning your retirement...

Chapter 9 – The end of the journey?

You can be young without money, but you

can't be old without it.

~Tennessee Williams

So we're finally coming to what some would consider as the final landmark on your journey - your retirement.

Or is it?

Should we see retirement as the end of the roadmap or is it the beginning of a new one? After all, if the success is in enjoying the journey rather than the destination, then surely this is just another life stage to plan for along the way – albeit quite a long life stage!

The other thing I would like to point out regarding retirement is that it is not based on how old you are. It's based on your financial position. If you've looked after you finances correctly over the years then it's highly likely that you will be able to retire earlier than someone who hasn't.

In reality, you can afford to retire when you have enough, not when you're old enough. The question here, however, is therefore 'how much is enough'?

This is what we will try to answer in this chapter.

Whilst retirement is often achieved in our later years (the reason being that it can take you 40 years of savings to fund it) the fact is that we are all living longer these days thanks to medical advances, improved social care and better lifestyles and diet. For some people this means that they could have a 40 year career followed by a 40 year retirement!

You may think this is a little too optimistic, but do you know the age group that's experiencing the fastest growth in the UK? Centenarians. That's right, people living past 100!

From the 1950's onwards the number of centenarians in England and Wales has increased at a faster rate than any other age group.

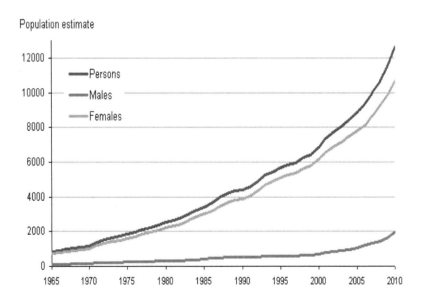

Population aged 100 years and over, UK, 1965-2010

Source: Office for National Statistics

Over the period from 1911 to 2008 it is estimated that the number of centenarians has increased 95-fold from only 100 in 1911 to 9,600 in 2008.

The major contributor to the rising number of centenarians is increased survival between the age of 80 and 100 due to improved medical treatment, housing and living standards, and nutrition.

Your retirement is not determined by your age. It's determined by your financial position.

Have you noticed that in the graph above over 10,000 of the 12,000+ centenarians were women? I asked a doctor why he thought this was and he answered "when you've been married for that long it's probably by choice that the men go first!" Hey hang on ladies; they were his words not mine!!

Now I personally think that it's great news that we're living longer, I genuinely do. I'd love to live to age 100 even if it's just to get my kids back for all the costs of looking after them. However, there is a problem that comes with being retired for as long as you've worked and it's this...

HOW THE HECK ARE YOU GOING TO AFFORD IT?

Let me hit you with the real facts now about the current state of the pension system in the UK-

There may not be enough workers to pay pensions in the future.....

The baby boomers are retiring. That's right, the UK's largest generation (in terms of numbers) are collecting their state pensions from around now. Now these baby boomers didn't have as many children as the previous generation so the proportion of taxpayers to pensioners is falling rapidly.

What does that mean? Well put simply, there will be less workers under 65 paying in to the state pension scheme and more pensioners collecting it, and for longer.

In 1941 there were 5.6 workers for each pensioner, in 2000 there were about 4 workers per pensioner and by 2040 it's estimated there will be just 2.6.

In the short to medium term, the Office for Budget Responsibilities has estimated expenditure forecasts for unfunded public sector pensions is expected to reach £9.4 billion in 2014-15, up from £3.1 billion in 2009-10. As a share of nominal GDP, this amounts to a rise from 0.2% to 0.5%.*

*source; public sector liabilities – improving transparency Working Study Paper July 2010

Final Salary Pension Schemes are in Massive Decline.....

Employers are switching from the secure (for members) final salary pensions where the required employer contributions were around 20% to money purchase schemes where the average contribution is only 10%.

The governments' new legislation on the workplace pension scheme (or 'NEST') will soon make pensions contributions compulsory but the maximum contributions required from the employer is only 3%.

Pension funds have struggled since the millennium with 3 major stock market corrections

For the 10 years up to May 2009 equity returns averaged just 1.3% a year – lower than cash and bonds. This means that the funds haven't grown as well as expected leaving less in the pot to fund the members' lifestyle needs.

People are living longer

We've already seen the statistics on how we're living longer. When the state pension was created the average age of death for a man was 67 and now it is 84 (a recent Paternoster study said that half of today's 30 year olds could live to age 100). This means that the state pension will be paying benefits to people for much longer.

Annuity rates are at a historic low

Another current issue is the fact that annuity rates, which determine how much you will get as a pension each month from your pension fund, are closely aligned with interest rates and gilt yields. And guess what? These have been relatively low for a long period – meaning that the income you get from your pension fund is substantially lower than someone who started taking their pension benefits 20 years ago, even with the same fund.

As at April 2013 a single life, level annuity for a 65 year old man with a pension pot of £100,000 would pay an income of just £5804 a year*. In 1990, the same level of savings bought an income of £15,640, over 160% higher than today.

*Source webline, April 2013

All of these facts add up to one simple conclusion – we have a potential pension time bomb on our hands!

What do you mean, pension time bomb?

Well in March 2009 Aegon SE conducted a retirement research of 1425 people in the UK between 30 and 65. This is what they found...

- 2/3rds of people admit they are not saving enough for their retirement - yet 2/3rds are also gambling each week on the lottery, bingo and the pools

- 30% of people felt they will need between £15-20,000pa to live comfortably in retirement. To provide an income of this size from a personal pension you would require a pension fund of almost £200,000 - yet the average annuity purchased in 2009 was approx £1500pa with an average pot of £25000

- A quarter of people between the ages of 30 and 40 admitted they would reduce their pension contributions before reducing luxury expenditure if they had budget constraints

Want some more?

- The Department of Working Pensions estimates there are around 7 million people who are not saving anything or not saving enough to generate the type of income they are likely to want or expect in retirement

- 87% want to retire on an income greater than £10,000 pa yet 40% of those questioned on this admitted to having no pension savings at all

Aegon's survey concluded –

"It would seem many people are unaware how much money they need to protect their families and plan a comfortable retirement and have little comprehension of their actual future financial needs.

Even though people are aware they are not planning enough for their future financial security, the research also reveals a third of respondents are unwilling to seek proper financial planning and advice. It is those people who are at most risk of facing financial poverty in retirement."

The report was entitled 'A Rose Tinted Future?'

OK, so that's the current situation. Can you see why it's called a pension time bomb now? We have a problem don't we?

Yes but surely the government will sort all this out won't they? Surely they could just print more money and give it to the pensioners? Surely they will increase taxes so there's enough in the pot for everyone? Err...well I don't think that will happen. For a start if they increased taxes it's you who will be taxed!!!

One of the things the government has done to attempt to reduce the financial effect of this is to increase the state pension age. Between 2010 and

2020 women's retirement ages are increasing to 65. Between 2024 and 2026, retirement ages for men and women are increasing to 66. Between 2034 and 2036, retirement ages for men and women are increasing to 67. Between 2044 and 2046, retirement ages for men and women are increasing to 68.

As mentioned above, legislation has also been introduced in The Pensions Act 2008 to create something called workplace pension schemes. This established new duties for UK employers from 2012 to provide some or all of their workers with access to a workplace pension scheme that meets certain legal requirements. Employers will have to automatically enroll certain workers into a **qualifying pension scheme** and pay contributions on their behalf.

However, despite these efforts, one thing that remains constant in any form of financial planning (especially retirement planning) is this - you're still going to have to take charge of this responsibility yourself.

If you don't want to suffer the chance of poverty in old age then you have to be willing to do something about it. I'm afraid only long standing members of certain employers pension schemes such as the police, the NHS, teachers etc can still feel safe about their retirement – and how long that will last no-one knows!

So how can you take responsibility and what can you actually do to ensure you retire on time and on target?

Well here's a 7 step process below that should help...

Oh, quick note before we start on the retirement planning process. What

I'm going to focus on here is mainly retirement planning through the use of pension plans. I'm not saying that this is the only method you can use. In fact there are many alternatives to funding for your later years. This could

If you don't want to suffer the chance of poverty in old age then you have to take the responsibility of planning it yourself.

be buying rental properties, selling your business, downsizing, equity release, using other investment products etc. However, as pension plans obtain tax relief and are a popular way of planning for retirement I will stick to this for now. Should you be using any of the other methods then try to calculate the income they will generate and then include them in the planning examples below. It's exactly the same principle anyway.

OK, so how do we start?

1. Begin with the End in Mind

Unless you've just opened this book by chance at this page, you've probably realised by now that financial planning always begins with goal setting (lifeline) then moves onto financial planning and budgeting (crunching the numbers) before looking at financial advice (using the right products).

I explained the 'Beginning with the end in mind' theory in chapter 1. This is where the late Stephen Covey states in his book 'The 7 Habits of Highly Successful People' that "all things are created twice. There's a mental or first creation, and a physical or second creation".

So when it comes to retirement planning I want to recommend you put down the book, close your eyes and then imagine yourself in retirement. Go on, this should be fun. What will you look like? Young fella's, will you keep your hair? The six pack? Older fella's, will you keep your marbles?

On a more serious note, who will you be spending it with? What would you like to spend your time doing? On a sunny Wednesday afternoon, what will you be choosing to do if you have enough income to pay for it?

Finally, ask yourself this question too...***when*** will it be? 55? 60? 65? 70? Never?

By establishing a date you give yourself the distance you're travelling and the time to arrive there, just like in our journey. Without this, it will be hard to know how much fuel you will need and how to establish the best route.

The funny thing is, we do all of this for our annual holidays already. We plan a date when we want to go. We have an image in our head of how we want it to be and where we want to go. We then try and find something that ticks all of those boxes within a budget that we can afford. It's a very similar process isn't it? When....what....how much?

The sad fact is that most people spend more time planning their annual holiday than they do when planning for the longest holiday they will ever have – their retirement. Instead they bury their head in the sand and hope everything will be OK. Let me tell you, if that's what you're doing, then it won't just turn out OK and YOU will be one of the people mentioned in the survey that will be at a high risk of facing poverty in retirement.

Depending on your age now, retirement may seem a long way off, yet I still think you need to create your retirement lifestyle in your mind NOW. Remember, this will be the longest day off you ever get so it's worth painting the picture in your mind of how you'd like to spend it. Remember the old saying "if you don't know where you're going you might not like where you end up"! Well with retirement if you don't get a plan in place there's a strong chance you won't like where your final destination will be too!

If you're finding it difficult to create a vision of what you want your lifestyle in retirement to look and feel like try it from a different angle and ask yourself 'what do you NOT want it to look like'?

Would you like it to be difficult to pay the bills? Would you like to have to sell your home and downsize? Would you want to cut out luxuries you're used to today? Would you like to work way past the age you'd like to? Or your body wants to if you have a physical job?

In my experience, when having these discussions with clients, I often find that many people don't have a clear idea of what they want in retirement. However, when we talk about what they don't want, things become much clearer. And what none of them want is this - an inferior lifestyle to the one they have now.

So, if you can't think of what you want then try and plan to maintain what you have now. With this in mind let's move onto step 2.

2. Work out what will it cost to do the above?

A good way of estimating the cost of your retirement is to look at your current expenditure (that you hopefully completed in Step 2 – Establishing your Budget). That should show you how much 'life' is costing you today.

You then need to work out what you think will happen to each expenditure item when you retire. For example we can presume that your mortgage payment may not be there anymore, your children's expenses may be gone, and the money you've been putting away for your retirement is probably now free to spend? On the other hand you may want to increase your holiday expenditure, protect against long term care issues, perhaps you will have to care for elderly parents etc?

The end result of this is that you should end up establishing the percentage of your current expenditure you will require in retirement – and this is what you can start to base your planning on.

Example – your current household income is £2000 (after tax) and your expenditure is £1700 - of which £300 is for your mortgage, £200 is for children's expenses, £200 is for your pensions and savings and £200 is for your holidays. Let's assume that your goal is to maintain your current standard of living when you retire but increase your expenditure on holidays by £100 per month.

The analysis will look like this –

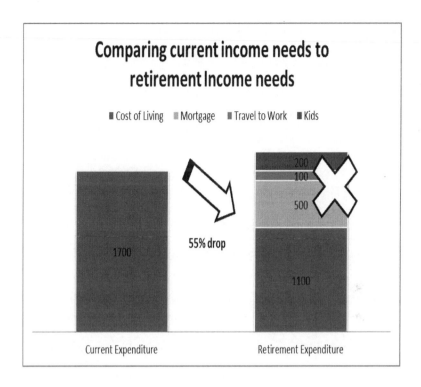

Current expenditure = £1700

Retirement expenditure requirement = £1100 (£1700 minus £300 mortgage minus £200 children's expenses minus £200 savings + £100 for extra travel costs)

So, in this example the income you would require in retirement is therefore 55% of your current income (1100(retirement expenditure) divided by 2000 (current expenditure) x100).

Once we have this figure of the percentage income we need to maintain our lifestyle in retirement we can move onto step 3.

3. Establish what is in place already

If you have a final salary pension scheme (where your retirement income is based on the number of years' service and your final salary) then you will get a statement every year telling you what your retirement income should be. You need to factor this in to your calculations. It's the equivalent of knowing what's in the petrol tank already.

If you have a private pension then you will get a retirement forecast from your pension company, not all of these will give you a projection to retirement so you will have to ask your pensions company, or your adviser that helps you with your pension.

A projection will show you the projected value of your pension fund at different growth rates (usually at 5%, 7% & 9%). To be cautious, you could use the projected figure at 5%, the more optimistic can use 7% and the ambitious can use 9%.

Underneath those figures it will also project what the tax free cash will be at your chosen retirement age (will usually be 25% of the total fund) together with the income (or annuity) that you could expect to receive.

These figures need to be factored into your retirement plans – and if you're a couple that intends to be together in retirement then you need to get both sets of figures. It's effectively like looking at the fuel gauge.

The other thing to consider is what your state pensions will be. I've mentioned already that the state pensions are becoming accessible later in life for many people but they will play a big factor in your retirement income for all but the very wealthy (if they're still available when you retire!).

There is a form called a BR19 that allows you to get a forecast from the government of what your state pension will be. Alternatively, if you go online you can get one now from www.direct.gov.uk website.

Once you've completed this request, again, you can add the figures into the pot so your retirement planning image will start to look like this...

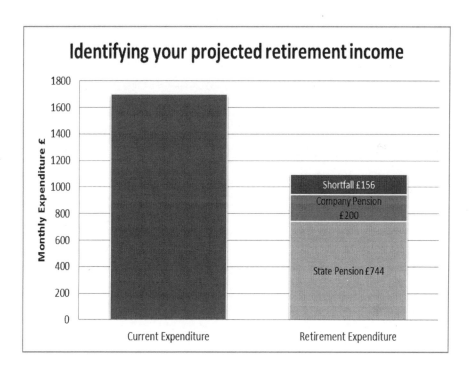

Identifying your projected retirement income

4. Calculate the fund required to generate the shortfall (if any).

Firstly, remember that the state pension will cover part of your spending (unless you intend on retiring earlier than that). The current maximum weekly rate, as at 2013-2014, is £110.15 for a single person with an extra £66 for a married man or woman/civil partner who is using their partners National Insurance record. That's the equivalent of £477 per calendar month if you're single and £763 if you are a couple.

So, in the example above, a married couple that needs £1100 per month in today's money will have a shortfall of £337 per month when you take off the state pension (£1100 minus £763=£ 337).

To generate an annuity of £337 per month (that escalates with inflation) a 65 year old will need to have a pension fund of around £67400. (An annuity is a guaranteed monthly income that is paid out by a pension company).

How did we arrive at the £67400 you may ask?

A very basic way of establishing how much you will need in your pension pot currently is to assume an annuity rate of 6% (the amount per year you will receive from the fund when you buy an annuity) and work back therefore to the fund required. The figure above of £337, when multiplied by 12 to get the annual figure, is around 6% of £67400.

To get this via a calculator just type in Monthly shortfall (337) times 12 (to get the annual shortfall) divided by 6 (approximate annuity rate) times 100 (to get the fund required).

However, don't forget you may also be liable for income tax on whatever your pension arrangements generate AND we have not taken into account any allowance for the tax free cash that can be taken out of a pension immediately.

Tax free cash is currently limited to 25% of the fund so this means you will need, in broad figures, 25% more than the £67700. This means you will need a fund of around £90000 to generate the £337 per month.

You can work this backwards by typing in £90,000 (your pension fund) times 75% (to take out the tax free cash) times 6% (annuity rate) divided by 12.

So, if you have a shortfall of £1000 per month you will need a fund of around £250000, after any tax free cash, when you take income tax into account. Here's a question. How many of you reading this have a pension fund of £250,000? If you're nodding then congratulations, you're in a small minority.

Current research states that the average private pension pot is around £30,000. If this is correct then this means that, after tax free cash, the 'average' pension pot holder can expect a pension income of £112.50 per month at 65 from their pension fund. Is that enough?

Also, 6% is a relatively reasonable figure to use as at 2013 for someone age 65. If you want to retire younger than 65 then you will need to reduce this as the annuity rate drops slightly for each year earlier that you want to retire. This is because the annuity providers, or pension companies, assume you will be receiving the benefits for longer so they will have to pay more out over time. If you want to find out what rates are available is quite easy. Simply type 'annuity rate at age (input the age)' into google and you will soon find the current annuity rates for that age. If it says 5% (maybe you put in annuity rates at 55) then re do the calculations at 5%.

Another thing to be aware of is that the annuity rate will change based on how you want to take benefits. When you buy an annuity there is a myriad of choices on how you can take the benefits. Do you want it increasing each year? Would you like it to be paid for a minimum period of time, say 5 or 10 years, even if you die during that term? Would you want your spouse to receive half of your pension income for their life if they outlive you?

I think it's fair to say that I could write a full chapter (at least) on taking retirement benefits. Not only are there lots of choices on how to take your annuity but there is an increasing number of other choices available now that allow you to take pension benefits without even buying an annuity for life. Options known as 'drawdown' or 'phased retirement' have become available, as have different types of investment related and/or flexible forms of annuity.

If you are reading this book and you are approaching your planned retirement I would suggest that you start to read up on all these options so you can make the right decision. After all, if you get it wrong you could end up regretting it for 40 years! If you're still a fair distance away from your planned retirement then I would suggest that your focus should be on accumulating the assets to fund it in the first place.

The reason why we need so much in the way of savings to survive is that, on average in Britain, a man will now live for 17 years more after retiring at 65, while a woman will live for nearly another 20 years. According to a report by the Centre for Economics and Business Research, if you are one of the increasing numbers of people who live to 100, you will have spent a total of £708,500 after retiring — because of the way inflation works. In real terms, the amount you spend drops as you age, but the actual cash you need rises, as inflation pushes up the price of almost everything.

The study, commissioned by Life Trust, says that in the early years of retirement (when people are still in their 60s) spending on recreation, culture and transport are the biggest items in the budget.

If you get your retirement decisions wrong you could end up regretting it for 40 years!

Retirees typically spend £5,000 a year on recreational activities, such as cinema tickets, theatre and home entertainment equipment.

By the time you reach 85, your total weekly spend is expected to rise by £366 (which takes into account inflation), with a large proportion going on housing, fuel and power costs (25%). After that, spending on healthcare and domestic help increases – but clothes spending drops to just 1% of the typical budget.

http://www.thisismoney.co.uk/pension-pot-calculator has a simple tool to help you work out what size pension pot is required if you want to try and plan your pension funding alone.

So, now you know when you want to retire, how much it will cost and how much you need in the fund to achieve it, the next stage is to......

5. Work out how much you need to save to generate the required fund.

The golden rule here is this – the earlier you start saving for your retirement the less you have to put away per month. What I come across regularly when talking about pension planning is that the younger age groups say 'I don't want to put too much in' and the older age group say 'I wish that I'd put more in' - typical human nature that isn't it? It's just like when we put a fiver on a horse, if it wins we always say I wish I'd put a tenner on it now! By the way, I'm not advocating gambling, gambling is bad, repeat BAD for your finances...unless you're a bookmaker!

The way to establish the contribution level required to meet the fund required can be complicated as you need to take into account things such as your age, your needs, your current fund, your current contributions, any employer contributions, fund growth etc

Luckily I know how you can make this a little easier. Go to google and type in 'pension retirement calculator' and look through the sites. If this one is still available when you're reading this book then go to http://money.guardian.co.uk/calculator/form/0,,603163,00.html and fill in the details.

This is a free and easy to use calculator (and still available as at July 2012 at least). Once you've done it you may want to sit down for a minute. Maybe have a nice cup of tea? That's always a good remedy for a nasty shock! Unfortunately, planning for a good retirement doesn't come cheap.

6. Apply your investment strategy

I won't go into much detail here as we covered it in the last chapter but you need to plan your portfolio around the level of risk you are willing to take and the amount of money you need to accumulate. For example, let's say that you need to contribute £300 per month to your pension to achieve the fund you need at 7% growth ***but you can't afford it.*** Well you have a few choices –

1. Accept it and just retire later

2. Accept it, still retire at your chosen age on a lower income and reduce your expenditure in retirement

3. Attempt to reduce the charges on your contract in the hope that will increase the fund

4. Take more risk with your pension fund to attempt to grow the fund faster

5. Marry someone rich!

Right now I wouldn't be surprised if there's a few of you wanting to opt for the latter!

If you're adamant, however, that you don't want to retire later or reduce your lifestyle in retirement (and marrying someone rich is not a viable option) then you can look at reducing your charges on your pension fund and/or taking more risk with the funds you have to try and seek a higher return.

Planning for a good retirement doesn't come cheap.

We have covered how you can adapt your portfolio to take more (or less) risk in the chapters on saving and investing so, at this point, we will look at how to reduce your pension charges.

The charges on your pension fund are highlighted by something called the reduction in yield. Put simply the *reduction in yield* is the cost of running your pension plan and it's shown by calculating what the net return is from the gross return.

If you look through your latest pension quote (and sometimes your latest pension statement) your reduction in yield could show something like this;

Contribution type	Mid Investment Growth Rate	Growth rate after deductions
Transfer payment	7%	5.6%
Monthly premium	7%	5.6%

Here we see that, for every 7% your pension makes, you will receive 5.6% as the costs of running the scheme and paying the parties involved such as an adviser, the fund manager, the pension company etc equates to 1.4%.

Analysing different providers' reduction in yield figures will allow you to compare the costs of each scheme. In theory, if two pension funds return the same level of growth but one has a better (or lower) reduction in yield then you will receive a higher fund from this, as less has been taken out to run the scheme.

However, as in anything, lowest cost doesn't always mean best value. The real skill is in choosing a low cost provider with funds that produce a good net return. It's better for you to have a gross return of 10% with a 4% charge than a gross return of 6% with a 1% charge. I say skill, though in reality it's really skill mixed with good fortune. No-one knows who will be the best performer really, despite what some 'experts' claim.

Without a doubt, the best option for improving your retirement lifestyle is to work on a combination of putting the right amount in to a low cost, high performing retirement plan as early as possible. Do that and you give yourself the best chance of avoiding poverty in old age.

7. Monitor It

The most common mistake I see with pension planning is this - a client gets it in his head that he needs to start retirement planning so says to an adviser "I want to contribute X amount per month as that's what I can afford". The adviser, not thinking about the end result, fills in the application form and off he goes. 7 years later the client is starting to build up a steady pension fund but all he gets is a statement once a year that he doesn't understand so he puts it in the file where he keeps everything else that looks important but doesn't understand.

I'm not being condescending here about the lack of understanding by the way; I'm actually saying that the insurance companies don't help with the way they communicate. I've seen documents that I've had to read several times to understand what they're saying - and I'm supposed to know!

Anyway, the final key to good retirement planning (once you've set it up correctly) is to MONITOR THE PROGRESS ANNUALLY. If you relate it to a journey and retirement is your final destination then you need to keep an eye on the petrol gauge together with the number of miles left to make sure you don't run out of fuel. That's the same idea with retirement planning. You need to know the number of years to your retirement, what the final pension fund needs to be and how much is in your pension pot today to establish whether you're on track. Some years you will have good performance which will get you there faster but some years the investment may perform poorly and this will slow you down (let's call them road works !!!)

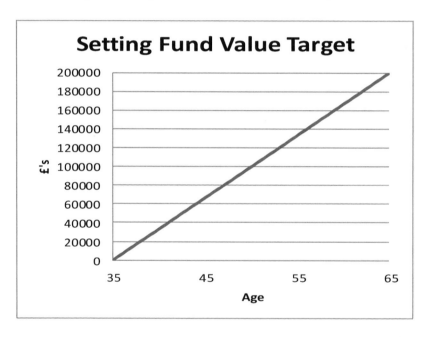

A simple way of monitoring is to chart your progress on a simple graph. For example, if you're 35 and plan to retire at 65 and need a fund of £200,000 to generate the income required to meet your shortfall, then it would look something like the previous chart.

Once you have this template then you can chart your fund progress each year by placing the fund value from your annual statements on the chart like this:-

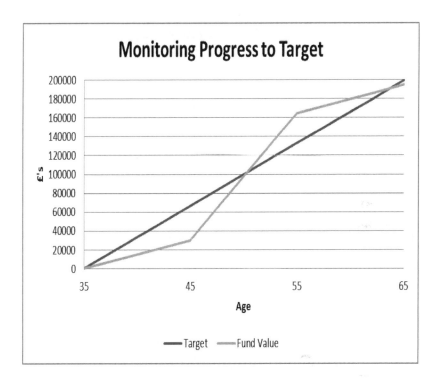

Having a progress chart like this will help you to stay on track and make appropriate decisions each year. It's far better than doing what the vast majority of people do, which is to file their annual statement away and have no idea what it actually means until they get to retirement age. Not burying your head in the sand when it comes to retirement planning is the key.

Is this your retirement strategy?

To summarise –

1. **Begin with the end in mind**

   Make a plan for your retirement date and create a vision of how you would like your life to be when retired.

2. **Work out the Cost**

   Calculate the annual cost of this lifestyle by comparing it to your current monthly or annual expenditure sheet.

3. **Establish what's in place already**

   Understand your pension statements and identify what the government will be providing in terms of state pensions.

4. **Work out the fund required to meet the shortfall**

   Based on an annuity rate of 6% a £1000,000 pension pot will give you £6000 per annum (ignoring the tax free cash you can take from your pension). So, if you need £24000 per year in retirement and you estimate that £6000 of this will come from the state pension then you will need a fund of £300,000 to give you the other £6000.

5. **Work out how much to save**

   Go online and find a retirement calculator that will show you how much you need to save each month to achieve your desired fund. http://money.guardian.co.uk/calculator/form/0,,603163,00.html is a good one.

6. **Have an investment strategy**

   Chapter 7 covers this in more detail but essentially you will need to decide how much risk to take based on the amount you will be paying and the term of years to retirement

7. **Monitor**

   A long term savings plan has a lot of time for things to change – for good and bad. By monitoring your progress on an annual basis you will be able to make the necessary changes to keep you on track. It's a bit like checking your petrol gauge and comparing it to the number of miles left on your journey.

OK, just some more chapter to go now and you will have your very own comprehensive financial plan. We just need to cover the importance of monitoring your progress.

Chapter 10 – Review/Monitor/Amend

Evaluate what you want -- because what gets measured gets produced.

~James Belasco

Well here we are at the final step of our 10 Steps to Financial Success program.

Before I move on to the final step I would like to do one final recap on each step in the series and remind you of the basics we covered.

Chapter 1 was about 'Creating your Lifeline' and covered the initial dreaming/goal setting process. This was done by identifying the events and life stages you want or need to plan for, placing them on your lifeline and then establishing the likely costs. I compared this to planning a long car journey before you set off so you know where you're going, which route to take, where to stop on the way, how much fuel you will need for the journey and how long it will take to get to your destination.

Chapter 2 was about 'Establishing your Budget'. Here we created an inventory of your outgoings, analysed where we could make savings or change our habits in order to release more money than can be used towards the goals established in Step 1.

In chapter 3 we talked about the value and purpose of having a net worth statement.

Chapter 4 was 'The Importance of an Emergency fund'. Having an emergency fund is important because it enables us to stay on track even when minor obstacles get in our way. Be it an illness, a redundancy or even just a broken down boiler an emergency fund enables a quick fix to the solution so that it doesn't become a disaster.

Chapter 5 was 'Ditch the Debt' and was all about the burden that debt can create, the way it slows you down from reaching your goals and how you need to plan to avoid the debt cycle.

Chapter 6 – 'Build a House of Stone' was then all about protecting against more serious setbacks or even catastrophe's such as death/critical illness etc. Even the best laid plans can come unstuck when a wolf comes to 'huff and puff' against what you are building.

Chapter 7 was where we eventually set off on 'the journey' to reach your goals. It discussed the issues of saving towards each objective on your landline, calculating the investment required and then which products to use based on whether the goal is in the near, medium or long term future.

We then moved on to savings 'bigger brother' in chapter 8 – Investing - where we talked about following an investment process. This included identifying the investments purpose, the level of risk you're willing to accept, the concept of asset allocation and correlation between asset classes, the choice of tax wrapper, investment style and product provider (yea, it was a heavy one!!).

In chapter 9 we covered retirement planning and, so, here we are at the end of the long and winding road eh?

Well actually, no we're not.

For example, take this car that we've been doing our journey in. Do you think it will run forever without looking after it? Of course not, every 6000 miles or so you will probably service it. If your car is over 3 years old the government will force you to get an M.O.T. to make sure it's road worthy. You will constantly have to make sure the engine has oil and that all its components are working safely. If not it could lead to some major expense or, even worse, a nasty accident. Occasionally you will have to change the tyres to avoid a potential blow out.

And that's just the same with financial planning because, just like our car trip, financial planning is a journey not a destination. The success is not necessarily in the achievement, it's in the achieving. It's in the fact that having a purpose and a goal and then marrying your money to that purpose is what creates financial harmony. Hopefully, this leaves to a correct balance and, ultimately, peace of mind.

One of my sayings about financial planning is "It's not about your money; it's about your life". This is not just a wordy gimmick to me, it's a philosophy I believe in.

You see if making money was all it was about then why do you see multi-millionaires committing suicide? On the other side of the coin why do some very wealthy people continue to work hard? Well if

Having a purpose and a goal and then marrying your money to that purpose is what creates financial harmony.

it's because they feel that 'just one more million' will be the secret to their happiness then I'm afraid they're wrong. If it's because they have a worthy goal that drives them to continue building something that will leave a positive mark, secure their kids future or even just keep them active then I think it has a better chance.

Hey, if they're working hard so they can give more away to their local church or other worthy causes then fantastic. I mean, how great would it be if we all had enough money to fulfil our needs that we could then start to focus on helping others less fortunate?

Anyway, back to the 10 Steps. Where are we? Oh yeah, back at the beginning!! We're back at the beginning because financial planning is not a one-off event. It's a constant monitoring, evaluating and adjustment process.

Charles Coonradt who was the founder of The Game of Work said ***"You have to measure what you want more of"***. He goes on to explain that successful people do this because ***scorekeeping stimulates us to create more of the positive outcomes we're keeping track of and so reinforces the behaviour that created these outcomes in the first place.***

Can you remember when you were a kid and you used to count how many marbles you'd won in the school playground? (yeah I know it was a long time ago but I remember anyway). Did your parents ever stand you against a door so they could measure your height against it and put the date at the side?

You see, when we want more of something it does come quite naturally to want to measure this because, basically, it makes you feel good when you see the growth doesn't it?

So how do we measure the success of our financial plan? Well here's some tips....

1. Invest an hour each month analysing your income/expenditure to see how much of your income has been allocated towards your goals and what you're spending habits are. Check through your bank statements, consolidate them by cross checking your expenditure with your statement. You could also analyse if you have any money left at the end of the month that can be used towards one of your goals. Your expenditure can vary quite substantially month to month and it's important to capitalise on any spare monies you have on a low expenditure month.

2. Check the value of your investments quarterly and then adjust your net worth statement accordingly.

3. Once a year undertake a full review of your plans.

Items I would recommend you cover in your annual review would be –

- A review of your original goals and how relevant they still are

- Any new goals/events that need to be planned for

- An overview of your income and expenditure to see if savings have been and can still be made

- An assessment of the performance of your investments to see if you are still on target

- Keep up to date with corporate/tax or legislation changes to make sure the investments and products you are using are still appropriate

- Re-do your attitude to risk questionnaire and then check the volatility of your funds to ensure it remains suitable

- Look at re-balancing your asset allocation in line with your attitude to risk score

- A monitoring of your net worth

- An overall progress check of how you are progressing towards your goals.

The importance of constantly monitoring can be likened to other vehicles that are on a journey. For example, do you know that a ship is very rarely on a direct line to its destination? The reason is the wind and tides are always subtlety affecting it, trying to push it off course. That's why the captain is constantly tinkering with the wheel in order to keep correcting it in order to stay on course.

It's the same with an aeroplane's autopilot system. It's constantly adjusting in order to stay on track. There's a car advert out at the moment that say's the wheels are making 500 decisions per second in order to stay in perfect contact with the road and make the ride smoother. 500 per second!

The point is this, setting up the plan on the right track is extremely important but then never reviewing can nullify its effect. If a ship's captain or an aeroplanes pilot just set it off on course without a constant monitoring programme in place then I'm pretty sure they would both end up somewhere quite different than they intended!

I often meet clients who reach retirement age and then say "I wish I would've done more with it but I've either not been looked after by my adviser" or "I just kept paying it and never really thought about it once I'd set it up." Unfortunately, most of the time, these clients are disappointed with the outcome.

Another example is the recent endowment shortfall debacle. Now I admit there were probably a lot of these policies sold without an explanation of the potential downside but when these plans started to reduce their bonuses, and thus reduce the final payouts, it coincided with interest rates falling. This meant that the monthly payments started to reduce on their mortgages. So, whilst they were not making the same returns on their investment they were benefiting by having lower mortgage payments. If these clients started to capitalise on the lower mortgage payments (by saving more or overpaying on the mortgage) then the shortfall's that have caused problems of late would have been mitigated.

OK, there's one final point I want to mention when it comes to the ongoing review of your financial plan and that is this – BE PATIENT & PERSISTENT.

This is probably one of the single most common qualities of high achievers.

Sometimes you may think things are progressing too slowly and sometimes you will suffer setbacks. In fact I tell my clients that investing is often a 3 step process – 2 will be forwards and then 1 backwards! In good times we may get 4 forwards and one backwards....in bad times it may be 2 backwards and one forwards...the fact is there will be always be the 'one backwards' sooner or later.

The key is to stay true to your vision and just keep tinkering with that steering wheel when you go off course. If you come to a roadblock then simply plan a detour. There is always an alternate course of action. You just have to find it.

> *Being patient and persistent is a quality of high achievers.*

Remember, Rome wasn't built in a day. In fact I believe that, what you can achieve or acquire quickly can also be lost quickly. That's why many of the lottery winners have gone bankrupt! You see, building a house of stone like we mentioned in chapter 6 may take longer but it will also last longer.

And, as your financial plan is for your life, surely you want it to provide the benefits for the whole of it?

So, there you have it. The final step of the 10 Steps, Review/Monitor/Amend has been covered and we have now finished the series.

I really hope you have found this book both informative and helpful. It has genuinely been my desire to give you practical information and guidance when it comes to managing your money. I also hope that I have kept the subject matter interesting and understandable, and haven't been too boring or technical. I realise some of my jokes weren't that great but I do get most of them from my kids so what can you expect?

All I can do now is to urge you to apply the principles we've been covering. Remember I said right at the beginning. This is not meant to be just a book you read on holiday. It's a practical step by step approach that only works when you apply the principles and do the work suggested.

Yeah I know some of it is a little boring (I admit, checking your bank accounts regularly is not going to be the most exciting part of your month) but it's worth the reward.

What's the reward? It's getting the best life you can with the money you've got.

So go on, get the best life you can.

Brian

How to get in touch with Brian

Brian can be followed on twitter @DoncasterIFAs.

He can also be emailed at brian@idealfinancialmanagement.co.uk

If you've read the book you may probably remember that I mentioned at the beginning that there are 3 enemies to financial planning-

1. Laziness

2. Ignorance

3. Fear of failure

In preparation that you may have read this book and thought 'yeah it would be great but I just can't get round to doing it (laziness) or 'I still didn't understand some of the principles (ignorance) or 'well it sounds great but I don't want to make any plans just in case they don't come to fruition (fear of failure) then I'd like to invite you to a

GET THE BEST LIFE YOU CAN WIH THE MONEY
YOU'VE GOT WORKSHOP

In this full day event you will

✔   Be taken through the 10 steps so that you have a full financial plan based on your needs and objectives

- ✓ Create your very own lifeline with all the anticipated costs factored in
- ✓ Create a budget and establish how you can save money and what can be used to achieve your goals
- ✓ Build your net worth chart
- ✓ Be given the worksheets to help you map out and calculate your lifeline needs
- ✓ Establish your attitude to risk so you can create your own investment strategy
- ✓ Establish what is required for an emergency fund
- ✓ Create a 'Get out of Debt' programme
- ✓ Ensure you have the right level of protection that is also cost effective
- ✓ Develop your own 7 step plan to retiring on time and on target

This full day's workshop with Brian will be fun and interactive. Spaces are limited to no more than 10 households (or individuals) and will include lunch and refreshments throughout the day.

The cost for this life changing day is only £145 for a single person or £195 for a couple. If you are a couple then I would always suggest (for maximum results and harmony in the home) that this program is done together, hence the reason for the large discount for the 2nd person.

When you take into account the fact that the average hourly rate for an IFA is £160* then a full day for £145 or £195 is great value.

*Research conducted by BDO accountancy of over 280 IFA's in 2012

At the end of the workshop you will leave with your very own comprehensive financial plan together with all the worksheets.

To further reduce the risk on your behalf there is also a money back guarantee that states, if you attend a full day's workshop and then don't feel it has returned a higher value than the cost, then you will get your money back.

So, if you feel this will assist you in putting your plans into action and will help you 'get the best life you can with the money you've got', then book on to a workshop by emailing brian@idealfinancialmanagement.co.uk.

It would be great to meet you.